Stand Down
The Camouflage of Racism

Dr. John I. Payne Jr.

Copyright © 2025 Dr. John I. Payne Jr.
All rights reserved. No part of this book may be reproduced by any mechanical, photographic or electronic process, or in a retrieval system, transmitted, or otherwise be copied for public or private use, without the prior written permission of both the copyright owner and the publisher of the book.

First Edition

MELANOID CREATIONS PUBLISHING
11603 Neon Road
Fort Washington, MD 20744

First originally published by Melanoid Creations Publishing 2026

ISBN 979-8-9935229-3-7 (Hardback)
ISBN 979-8-9935229-4-4 (Paperback)
ISBN 979-8-9935229-5-1 (Digital)
Library of Congress Control Number: 2026902837

Cover Design by Devin Coats of Emblem Marketing Solutions LLC. https://emblemsigns.com/contact-us/

Printed in the United States of America

DEDICATION

This book is dedicated to my namesake and first-born son, John I. Payne III. As the years pass, you will encounter many lessons that will shape your life. Your time in the Army will help you discover your place in the world and the role you are meant to play. I pray that you always put God first and embrace every positive opportunity that comes your way. Remember to live with good character and integrity—I am proud of the man you are becoming!

Love Dad

Table of Contents

DEDICATION .... *iii*

Foreword *1*

Introduction *4*

CHAPTER ONE 7
   ATTENTION TO ORDERS 7
      U-Haul Out Front 15
      A Request for Hardship 21

CHAPTER TWO 23
   FAVOR IS NOT FAIR! 23
      Back To Kansas 23
      MY TRIP THROUGH ALMA, KANSAS 29
      CSM Smith and Basic Non-commissioned Officers Course 37
      LAND NAVIGATION 39

CHAPTER THREE 52
   WHO'S LAUGHING NOW? 52
      Meet Your New Supervisor 52
      New Crew and Assignments 56
      Lead By Example 58

CHAPTER FOUR 69
   "The Gun Don't Fit" 69
      The Set-up Secured 74
      The Perfect Score 78

CHAPTER FIVE 118
   Enemies Become Footstools 118
      The Fallout 126

CHAPTER SIX 131
   A CHANGE IN PERSPECTIVE 131
      THE MEPS FAIRY 142
      MORNING CUP OF JOE 148

CHAPTER SEVEN 164

A CHANGE OF DUTY STATION 164
    Seventy-Nine Romeo 164
    Station Commander 172
    Right Place, Wrong Time... 174

CHAPTER EIGHT 180

THE FOLLOW UP... 180
    What Ever Happen to Thomas? 180
    Queen City Pit Stop 182
    Driving the Wrong Way... 187

CHAPTER NINE.. 196

Three Fifty-Seven 196
    Failed APFT 202
    Lawn Ritual 209

Friendship Bread 214
    Promotion Time 226

Foreword

At precisely 5:10a.m., August 9, 1969, at Orange Memorial Hospital, Orlando, Florida, God sat up on His throne and peeled back the veil of immortality and its divine order, and spoke to creation, and its ever-present cosmic chaos, while commanding the heavens to 'Stand Down," declaring that this battle is not Baby Martin's to own; and nor is it his to fight by his own might! He declared that what the devil had intended for bad, He would work things out for Baby Martin's good and wellbeing! The good, being the things that were yet to come, for a yet un-named, but already pre-destined infant, simply known as, Baby Martin.

Armed with the foreknowledge of knowing every follicle of hair on this newborn infant's head, every mountain he would have to scale, every valley he would descend, every river he would have to swim; God had already fought the battles and challenges of the heart that would test his faith of anonymity of the yet un-proven warrior-soldier. God in His Omniscience had already positioned and purposed Himself to do the 'heavy lifting' for Baby Martin. For inasmuch as Baby Martin's journey began in a shroud of mystery, inner turmoil of centimorgan mystique and a deep-seated longing to discover himself in his own soul, however, the war towards that reconciliation would be delayed until the Concealed God, became the Reveled God, as the General of the Universe, declared, "Be still and know, that I am your God..." (Ps 46:10) KJV. Stand Down! Although God's initial command to Stand Down wasn't directed at Baby Martin, who by divine design, had been born a warrior-soldier in every sense of the word of extraordinary caliber; thusly, in His infinite wisdom, God knew that ultimately, once Baby Martin's identity had been established and enshrined in the annals of governmental legalese as John Isham Payne, Jr., He would have to quell the warrior spirit in John, by dressing him in the full armor of God, so that He could fight every battle in victory for John to ensure that His will be done in John's life, while John Isham Payne, Jr., learned to obediently, wait patiently, and Stand Down! And as life would have it according to God's dictates, John I. Payne, Jr., evolved from mysterious and humble beginnings to become a gifted professional and accomplished military veteran, both a well-known and sought-after warrior-soldier on the speaker circuit; a man of great means and empathy, whose life's journey has impacted the lives of many on the world stage and from diverse backgrounds.

Then it should come as no surprise that God has led the author to pen, *"Stand Down!"* Coming on the heels of his highly successful, award winning, freshman offering, *"You May Not Be Who You Think You Are,"* John Payne's gift for writing provides us [the readers] another opportunity to glimpse the power, activity, and inner-workings of God in such a way that moves us to a closer relationship with God; a relationship that should cause each of us to diligently work towards understanding that God's purpose in our lives can and will be made manifest, if only we humble ourselves and Stand Down!

As you enjoy this book, I admonish you to understand that writing it wasn't John's idea or his choice, but rather, it was his decision, because God had already pre-destined it for him. And how befitting that he would trust God with such an assignment. Clearly, Baby Martin, aka John Isham Payne, Jr., personifies the essence of the Scripture that says, "…I have never seen the righteous forsaken, nor my seed begging for bread" (Psalm 37:25) KJV.

~Uncle-Daddy (aka Eddie Harris, Jr.)

Introduction

Stand Down: The Camouflage of Racism is not merely a memoir, nor is it solely a social critique. It is a testimony—of lived experience, earned wisdom, and hard truths revealed through service, sacrifice, and survival within institutions that profess equality while often concealing inequity beneath layers of tradition, authority, and silence. This book invites the reader into a deeply personal journey that spans decades of military service, leadership, faith, and reflection, while exposing the subtle and overt ways racism adapts, disguises itself, and persists.

At its core, *Stand Down* is about obedience—not blind obedience to flawed systems, but disciplined obedience to truth, character, and divine purpose. The title itself reflects a paradox familiar to every soldier: knowing when to advance and knowing when to stand down. Throughout these pages, the author wrestles with that tension, learning—often painfully—that strength is not always found in confrontation, and courage is not always loud. Sometimes, the most difficult command to follow is the one that requires patience, restraint, and faith in a justice greater than immediate vindication.

Through firsthand accounts of military life—from the barracks and the battlefield to the recruiting office and the command suite—this narrative reveals how racism rarely announces itself openly. Instead, it camouflages itself behind rank, policy, favoritism, and plausible deniability. It shows up in double standards, selective enforcement, weaponized authority, and the quiet complicity of those who benefit from not seeing it. Yet, this book does not paint its story in absolutes. It acknowledges complexity: allies who appear in unexpected places, adversaries who sabotage from within, and moments where integrity—not resentment—becomes the deciding factor between destruction and elevation.

Faith weaves through every chapter as both anchor and compass. The author does not present himself as flawless or infallible, but as a man shaped by trials that forced him to choose between bitterness and purpose. Scripture, reflection, and lived consequence intersect to form a recurring lesson: some battles are not won by force, but by surrendering control and trusting God to fight on your behalf. In those moments, the command to *stand down* becomes an act of spiritual warfare rather than weakness.

This book is also a leadership study—unfiltered and unapologetic. It challenges popular myths about meritocracy, neutrality, and "colorblindness," especially within systems that pride themselves on uniformity. It asks difficult questions: What happens when the very institutions designed to build character also test it unjustly? What does ethical leadership look like when power is misused? And how does one lead with integrity when the cost of doing so may be personal, professional, or permanent?

Ultimately, *Stand Down: The Camouflage of Racism* is written for those who have endured injustice without the luxury of outrage; for leaders who choose principle over popularity; for readers willing to confront uncomfortable realities; and for anyone seeking to understand how perseverance, humility, and faith can transform oppression into purpose. This is not a call to anger—it is a call to awareness, accountability, and growth.

As you turn the pages, you are not being asked to agree with every conclusion, but to listen. To see. And perhaps, to recognize that some of the most decisive victories in life are won not when we fight harder—but when we learn when, and how, to stand down.

CHAPTER ONE
ATTENTION TO ORDERS

ATTENTION TO ORDERS! The Secretary of the Army has reposed special trust and confidence in the patriotism, valor, fidelity, and professional excellence of John I Payne Jr. In view of these qualities and his demonstrated leadership potential and dedicated service to the United States Army, he is, therefore, promoted from Corporal to Sergeant. Promotion is effective 1 October 1992 with a date of rank of 1 October 1992.

After graduating from high school, I soon realized I was going nowhere fast, and enlisted in the U.S. Army. When I enlisted, I felt it was my last opportunity to make something of myself. Unlike many other Privates, I took my career seriously from the start. Although I did not make much money initially, I would iron my uniforms until there was no discernible difference between my efforts and the work of a professional dry cleaner.

Armed with a cotton diaper, black Kiwi shoe polish, and Honor Guard edge dressing, I would spit-shine my boots until they gleamed like polished marble. My mother always told me not to rush adulthood, which she expressed by saying, "John, don't rush to get grown, son."

Of course, like any child who figures he knows it all, I did not listen. At the tender and green age of nineteen, I did the unthinkable. I am still in disbelief at what I did more than thirty years ago.

I decided to get married at a young age. Because of the shame I felt from eloping, I did not share this embarrassing information with my mother. To add insult to injury, she figured it out after I forgot to take off my wedding band while visiting home.

The pain I felt from her disappointment was enough to make my heart feel as though it might stop. After a while, it appeared she got over it, but the pain for both of us lingered just beneath the surface for a few years.

Determined not to become a failure, I put all my energy into learning my military occupational skill and taking advantage of every opportunity for advancement. Throughout my military tenure, I read technical and field manuals—known as TMs and FMs—in the late 1980s and early 1990s, hoping for the opportunity to prove my worthiness to become a Non-Commissioned Officer.

All I could think about was someday becoming a Sergeant (SGT) and enjoying what I believed to be privileges reserved only for Non-Commissioned Officers, along with the pay that came with the promotion.

As I traveled on my journey toward authority, leadership, and pay, I met and befriended a like-minded soldier named John Prann. He and I gravitated toward each other because of our shared desire for advancement. He was from a town on the eastern seaboard of Maryland called Annapolis. Before meeting him, I had never heard of the city of Annapolis. Meeting Prann marked the first time in my life that I encountered someone as driven as I was. Together, we pushed each other to become the best at whatever obstacle stood before us. Prann and I began to do everything together. We studied, ironed our uniforms, shined our boots, and even exercised together in preparation for physical fitness exams.

Friendship is a funny thing; it is a lot like love. You never know if it is real until it is tested. Prann and I received a great deal of resentment from our peers as we ascended to the first level of Army leadership.

The day came when we were offered the opportunity to prepare for and attend a promotion board. Of the seven Specialists (SPC), only two accepted the challenge.

Yep, you guessed it—me and SPC Prann. The day Prann and I attended that promotion board was the same day we both suffered significant casualties in the friendship department.

It's strange how the elevation of some can cause others emotional heartburn. I learned a lot about friendship—and frenemies—during this time in my life.

After all the hard work to get there, the day finally came when I was promoted from Corporal (CPL) E-4 to Sergeant (SGT) E-5 on October 1, 1992. I cannot remember much of that day; however, I do remember a young man named John Prann standing next to me because he was also being promoted. We stood their side by side and received promotions we had worked hard to achieve.

Sergeant Prann provided me with an excellent example of the mental toughness I would need to lead others at a young age and become a successful Non-Commissioned Officer (NCO).

Along with my promotion to Sergeant, my previous two promotions were also shared with John Prann. The rank of Sergeant was a significant milestone in our lives, and we did not give up until we reached our goal.

One of the privileges of becoming a Sergeant is performing the duties of Sergeant of the Guard rather than guard duty itself. Looking back, both are pretty crappy tasks when compared to civilian life. Prann and I discussed in great detail how we would take advantage of our future duties and the enjoyment we expected once we no longer had to stand guard for hours in a forest somewhere in the world. Well, wouldn't you know it—Prann and I were promoted when the unit was short on soldiers to perform guard duty. As a result, we became the first Sergeants I had ever seen pulling guard duty instead of serving as Sergeant of the Guard.

I can remember the anger I felt as if it were happening at this very moment. Although he also had to pull guard duty, he showed far more composure than I did at the time. SGT Prann's ability to compartmentalize his emotions and demonstrate a high level of maturity was second to none.

After he delivered the bad news—which I considered as earth-shattering as the attack on Pearl Harbor—Prann patiently waited for me to cool down and then told me a joke. His joke was so funny that everyone who heard his voice inside the tent could not control themselves from laughter. Before telling the joke, Prann had to prep the audience—mainly me—because he wanted to take my mind off what I thought was the end of the world at the time. He said, "Sarge, let me tell you a joke!"

There was a guy who always wanted to own a candy apple red motorcycle. When he saved up enough money for a used bike, he went to the dealership. After explaining what he wanted, the dealer said, "I have exactly what you're looking for!" He pulled the motorcycle to the front of the dealership, and the guy took off on his test ride, dreaming about the fun he would have once the motorcycle was his.

After returning from the test ride, the guy quickly told the dealer he would take the bike. The dealer then explained that he was an honest salesman and could not complete the sale without disclosing one major flaw. The dealer said, "Son, this may sound a little strange, but under no circumstances can you allow this bike to get wet."

Then he said, "You must keep the bike lubed up with KY jelly, or it will rust really bad." Not to be discouraged, he purchased the motorcycle anyway, thinking to himself that this was a small price to pay for something he wanted so badly.

In anticipation of owning the bike, he purchased a black leather jacket with silver zippers and a lot of pockets. He had a dinner date with his girlfriend at her parents' house and could hardly wait to show her his new motorcycle.

On his way to pick her up, he stopped at the local drugstore, purchased a tube of KY jelly, zipped it into the pocket of his nice black leather jacket, and went on his way.

After arriving at her parents' house, his girlfriend stopped short on the porch and made a confession. She told him, "Look, my parents are very strange people. The first person to speak will have to wash the dishes! So, it is imperative that you not say a word while we're here."

He quickly agreed and rang the doorbell. Her parents opened the door, greeted them with hugs, and directed them to the family room to sit before dinner.

Soon afterward, they moved to the dining room table. The guy took a look into the kitchen and saw unwashed dishes stacked nearly to the ceiling. He said to himself, "I am going to make sure I do not breathe a word," for fear of becoming the one who would have to wash the dishes. Dinner was served, and everyone bowed their heads for silent meditation instead of praying aloud.

After dinner, the guy and his girlfriend joined her parents in the family room to watch television. The TV was situated directly in front of a large picture window in the center of the room.

While sitting there, the guy grew bored and began thinking of ways to get someone to talk. He started making out with his girlfriend in the presence of her parents, and no one said a word. When they finished, he kissed her mother, and still, no one said anything.

As he sat there watching TV, a large raincloud rolled in outside the window, and he suddenly thought to himself, "My bike!" He jumped to his feet, unzipped his jacket pocket, and pulled out the tube of KY jelly. The father immediately jumped to his feet and said, "OK, the joke is over—I'm washing the dishes!"

I know that wasn't a good joke, but we were immature 20-somethings and thought it was the funniest joke we had ever heard. After I regained my composure from laughing hysterically, Sergeant Prann said, "OK, Sarge, go to guard duty—you have the first shift!" I gathered my gear, walked to my post, and laughed internally during my entire shift. That day, John C. Prann taught me a valuable lesson: everything is mind over matter. If you don't mind, it doesn't matter—and vice versa.

I would later use his leadership style throughout my career to encourage and influence others to get the job done, whatever the task at hand. Not all situations require an authoritative leadership style to motivate soldiers to complete the mission.

U-Haul Out Front

There is a big difference between becoming an adult and what my elders would call becoming "grown." Like so many other young people, I graduated from high school by the skin of my teeth—I might add—and thought I was grown. Looking back now, I had no idea how the world worked, nor did I have a clue how to move about in it.

After several failed attempts to get off to a good start in life, I enlisted in the military. At the time, I believed it was my last opportunity to become someone.

On a warm and sunny September day in Florida, I departed for Fort Knox, Kentucky, to begin the unknown journey called basic training. The days passed quickly and left little time for reflection or reminiscing about life before becoming a soldier. Lights-out, however, was quite the opposite.

Lying in a dark, shared space with several other young men during mandatory bedtime allowed for self-reflection. That reflection was so intense I could hear my heart beating in my ears.

Anyone who has attended military basic training will agree that there is nothing better than breaking the ranks of a formation when your name is called to receive mail!

Receiving mail from family and friends was almost better than payday. My mother shared my information with a high school girlfriend during basic training. I could not wait until the end of the day, when the lights were turned out, so I could take out my flashlight and read the letters I received during mail call.

Basic training soon ended, and I was convinced I was grown—better yet, I was a "grown man." At the tender age of nineteen, I flew to Rochester, New York, to visit my high school girlfriend. She had relocated from Orlando, Florida, to be reunited with her mother after living with her father and his new wife while attending high school.

During what I believed would be a visit, I became convinced that my high school girlfriend and I should get married. Before I could think, my then-unwanted future mother-in-law set us on a one-way collision toward marital failure while simultaneously laying a secure foundation for her high school-dropout daughter. There I stood—green as a well-manicured blade of Saint Augustine grass—in a Monroe County courthouse, getting married. Oblivious to the fact that neither of us had experienced life enough to stop and consider what we had gotten ourselves into.

Eventually, the hurricane I found myself in subsided, but little did I know I was standing in the eye of the storm, unaware of the second wave yet to come.

A few years later, I found myself in Fort Riley, Kansas, as a young Sergeant with a failing marriage, preparing for a whirlwind of emotional events headed my way. This was the back end of the storm I was talking about earlier.

During the early '90s, I was a 19 Delta Cavalry Scout and the First Sergeant's driver. I can't recall how I received this position, which many other young Sergeants wanted. Still, I took pride in everything the position required and performed my duties very well.

As part of the job, my unit frequently participated in field exercises that mimicked a wartime environment to assess the unit's war-fighting capabilities and readiness. Sometimes we would be away for weeks at a time.

I have tried to recall the exact episode, and over time I have buried much of the detailed information deep in my temporal lobe, losing the ability to index as much of it as I would like. I guess it's my brain's way of protecting me from a once-traumatic event from the past. However, I remember the briskness in the fall air and the feeling that snow could fall at any moment.

It was my last day in the field, and I was elated to sleep under my own roof, take a shower, and do all the things I believed most civilians take for granted. Almost without fail, the conclusion of a long field exercise ended at the wash rack.

The wash rack in the Army is the equivalent of a car wash, apart from its design to accommodate large, tracked vehicles such as tanks and other reconnaissance vehicles. After a long and slow road march, the unit finally reached the wash rack.

No one enjoyed this, but it marked the beginning of the end of poor living conditions—sleeping in tents, pulling guard duty, and eating bad-tasting food for several weeks.

While most units were in the field, there were usually a few soldiers left behind on rear detachment, or what we called Rear D. Many of those soldiers were left behind for one reason or another, such as injury, illness, or a medical profile that prevented them from participating in long periods of living in the field.

Shortly after arriving at the wash rack, I was approached by a Sergeant who was on rear detachment. He said, "SGT Payne, you need to get to your quarters."

"I saw your wife and two guys clearing out your quarters and loading your furniture into a U-Haul."

I rushed to my quarters as fast as I could. When I arrived, I slammed my vehicle into park so hard it rocked back and forth. I jumped out and ran to the back entrance because it was closest to my designated parking space.

The door was left unlocked, and the window treatment I carefully installed with all the pride of a young husband was gone.

Briskly, I walked through an empty three-bedroom, two-story, single-family residence in shock. I slowed my pace as I climbed the stairs to the bedroom, only to find it empty as well, with trash and scattered papers covering the floor where my bed once stood.

I crept to my closet as if someone might be hiding inside. Slowly gripping the doorknob, I opened the closet door to reveal one of the loneliest images I have ever witnessed.

The only thing left in the entire house was my clothes hanging in the closet, just as I had last seen them a few weeks earlier before I left for the field. This moment remains at the top of my Mount Rushmore of painful events.

A Request for Hardship

After the finalization of my divorce, the air in Kansas became so thick it was hard for me to breathe, and I needed an escape to somewhere new to recharge and renew my spirit.

I called my branch manager and asked—actually begged—for a transfer to a different duty station. The Army has an acronym frequently used when it comes to re-enlistment and retention called IAW, which stands for "In Accordance With the needs of the Army." In my case, my branch manager could sense the desperation I was under and offered me a hardship tour to the Federal Republic of South Korea for twelve months. I accepted it without a moment's hesitation.

I never anticipated leaving a location faster than I prepared to leave Kansas. I remember praying never to have the misfortune of residing there again. Once the official documents touched my hands, leaving Kansas was a blur. My recollection resumes with me on a plane high above the planet, headed toward a new beginning. After arriving in Korea, it felt as though the sun had come out again.

It became a little easier for me to breathe despite the smell of kimchi and turtle ditches that made up the Korean landscape on many military installations. I was hopeful that a fresh start in a different location would improve my life.

While in Korea, I was able to pour myself into learning everything there was to discover about my military occupational skill. I even found time to take on a few additional duties as well.

As the days and months passed with me on foreign soil, I could feel my soul healing. I was transitioning from that naïve kid who left home believing everyone possessed common civility—something I could never shake—to a man with his eyes and ears wide open at all times.

I kept my head down and worked just as hard as I played. Before I knew it, my time was up. I was headed back to what us military people call, CONUS—the continental United States.

CHAPTER TWO
FAVOR IS NOT FAIR!

Back To Kansas

My return to the United States begins under the most unlikely of circumstances. In real-time I felt as if I was the most unfortunate soldier in the Army, but I later came to believe it was the favor of God!

The Army, in all its infinite wisdom, sent me back to the same exact place I had come from a year earlier. "For real—they sent me back to the same exact place," all the way down to the same unit on the installation.

After an overnight stay at the Dragon Inn Hotel in Seoul, Korea, I boarded a plane for the United States—more specifically, Orlando, Florida. I was looking forward to some well-deserved R&R in my hometown before making my way to my next permanent duty station. I can still remember the many emotions I felt as the plane descended into Orlando International Airport. It is the same mix of emotions I still feel to this very day whenever I get closer to home, regardless of the mode of transportation.

As the plane descended closer to the airport, I could barely sit still. The anticipation of going home caused my adrenaline to overflow and my heartbeat to quicken, and I grew more excited the closer I got to my parents' home.

I have had the pleasure of living in several places around the world, but there is nothing like the feeling of paradise or that special tropical atmosphere of living in Florida. There I was, back in the place of my birth, absorbing the sunrays, strong breeze, and visual stimulation of palm trees; well, manicured lawns with grass blades so thick you could use them to cut a steak; and a backdrop of blue skies with cumulus clouds that mimicked giant cotton balls.

The year I spent in Korea gave me the opportunity to save some money; however, it did nothing to improve the damage the divorce had done to my credit. I no longer owned transportation and pondered how I would get a car with such bad credit. My parents didn't have a whole lot, but whatever they had was always available to me if I needed it. Still unsure of how I was going to become a driving adult again, I borrowed my parents' vehicle and drove to a car dealership located on a popular main strip in my hometown called Colonial Drive.

For many years, my parents purchased their vehicles at the exact dealership I visited that day. Young and afraid, I drove slowly around the lot, choosing not to exit my parents' car. I feared a car salesman cornering me and asking questions about my intentions. I made every attempt to avoid talking to anyone because I knew I was over my head—I had never purchased a car on my own. I slowly drove around, passing one car after another, until I saw one that piqued my interest.

It was a 1988 teal-green, manual-shift Ford Mustang with a sunroof. I slowly pulled next to it and placed my parents' car in park before exiting the vehicle to get a better look.

The sun was at its highest, and nothing blocked it from shining as brightly as it ever had. I placed my hand across my forehead to shade my eyes so I could look inside what I believed was unobtainable at the time. Before anyone could approach me, I quickly returned to my parents' car and drove off the lot as I observed a salesman exiting the air-conditioned showroom heading in my direction. As I drove home, I began my strategic thought process—planning how to ask, or should I say beg, my parents for help if need be.

As soon as I walked through the door, my parents revealed to me that the dealership manager had called. He witnessed me admiring the Mustang, pulled it to the front near the showroom entrance, and requested that I return to the dealership for a test drive.

My parents and I quickly piled into their recently purchased mid-size white Ford Crown Victoria with the half-white vinyl top and headed back to the dealership I had visited only moments earlier. Because of the close proximity, we pulled back onto the lot not long after I had left. As we exited the car, a waiting salesman quickly made a copy of my driver's license, placed a dealer's tag on the vehicle, and handed me the keys for a test drive. I didn't go far on my test drive because I already knew—before leaving the lot—that I wanted that car more than anything I could remember wanting at that time in my life. I had already flashed forward and imagined myself as the happy owner.

First, however, I would have to figure out how to purchase this new car with bad credit, a divorce under my belt, and still many years away from celebrating my thirtieth birthday. It was only a few years earlier that I thought I was grown.

Now I had to humble myself and ask for help I believed I wouldn't need. I did not have the slightest clue how to go about purchasing this vehicle. Lucky for me, my stepfather had excellent credit and trusted me enough to co-sign the purchase, with the promise that I would make my payments on time and not damage his stellar credit in any way.

I drove off the lot that day with an innocence of happiness I had robbed myself of by wanting to grow up much faster than I needed to. I remember riding around, going nowhere, wasting gas as I got familiar with my new car. This was my first major purchase in more than a year. Although I was not completely out of the water, it felt good to get a win and receive some good fortune after living the life of a minimalist for the last few years.

My vacation moved at the speed of light, and before I could get used to being home, it was time for me to leave again.

I packed my clothes into my new car and prepared for my drive to the midwestern part of the United States, back to a place I was too familiar with—Fort Riley, Kansas.

After packing my new vehicle, I laid down for the night to ensure I was well rested for what I knew would be my longest road trip to date.

I awoke early, just as I was taught by my mother. It was unacceptable to head out on a road trip after sunrise. In her eyes, any person serious about life lived by the creed, *the early bird gets the worm*.

So, it was imperative that I get off to an early start. She called it *be-foe-day*, which means before day in the morning. I slept prepared to go, and my transition from waking, to dressing, to hitting the door was quite swift.

I have never done well with goodbyes, so I intentionally moved like I had a purpose. My mother held my hand and prayed for me before she would allow me to leave. We hugged each other, and my parents walked with me to the front yard to unlock the gate and release me back into the world. My stepfather unlocked the gate and removed the chain that held it together, providing them a level of comfort and security.

I started my car and slowly backed out of the driveway, placed it in first gear, and eased down the street while tapping the horn to offer them both a small token of acknowledgment.

In almost ceremonial fashion, I drove past the car dealership as the skyline of my hometown slowly disappeared in my rearview mirror. It seemed as if I was driving forever. Each town started to look like the last, and I had only my map, my music, and my thoughts to keep me company.

MY TRIP THROUGH ALMA, KANSAS

The hour would come when I crossed the border leaving Missouri and entered the state of Kansas. By this time, I had less road ahead of me, but still several hours of travel to conquer.

I noticed my fuel gauge was reaching the halfway mark and thought it would be a good time to get gas. I remember the fear I felt as I drove the open, dark, and unlit interstate without another car in sight.

In the distance, I could see the lights of a small town ahead. I slowed my speed and signaled as I merged off the interstate, hoping to get some gas and stretch my legs before continuing to Fort Riley.

A few yards up the road sat a gas station. However, I couldn't determine whether it was open from my current distance, so I proceeded with caution toward what turned out to be a two-pump gas station with very low lighting. As I pulled into the parking lot, I could clearly see it was closed.

I slowly drove through the lot past the pumps and back onto Main Street toward the interstate. Out of nowhere, a car pulled in behind me, and my heart began to race.

My heart was beating so hard I could hear it pounding in my ears. Checking my rearview mirror, I quickly noticed it was the police. My eyes moved back and forth between my rearview mirror and my speedometer. I wanted to make sure I was not speeding; I did not want to give the officer any reason to pull me over.

To avoid drawing any unwanted attention to myself, I eased my foot off the gas and slowed down without activating my brake lights. The few yards I needed to travel to get back to the highway seemed longer than all the road I had traveled to reach my current location.

The on-ramp was in sight, and my heart rate slowed a little as I began to feel somewhat safer the closer my car moved toward the interstate.

I started talking to myself, "You are almost there," as I-70 moved closer to my windshield.

While approaching the on-ramp, I engaged my turn signal and eased onto the interstate, merging cautiously even though there was no one on the road except the two of us. I recall taking a small sigh of relief.

Now that I was back on the interstate, I increased my speed, but the policeman was still behind me. My heart began to race again—this time almost to the point of hyperventilation.

Several miles from the small town, the police officer was still following me, and I was more frightened than I had ever been in my life up to that point. The lights from the police car were so bright they lit the inside of my vehicle as I drove down the highway. I began to think I would be killed in the middle of nowhere and that no one would ever find me.

My hands were locked on the steering wheel at the ten-and-two position, and the speedometer showed a full five miles per hour below the posted speed limit.

And then the unthinkable happened—the police officer turned on his rotating lights. His high-beam headlights reflected off my rearview mirror, bright enough to cause snow blindness.

Not comparing myself to civil rights icons but in that moment, I felt I would meet the same fate as the three civil rights activists who were murdered in Philadelphia, Mississippi, in 1964. The night was so dark that without headlights you could barely make out your hand if you held it directly in front of your face.

With nowhere to go, no light, and no one else on the road traveling in either direction, I slowly pulled to the right shoulder of the highway. I heard a voice come over the police car's intercom: "Shut off your engine."

I complied and quickly secured my driver's license, proof of insurance, and—hoping it would make a difference—my military ID card. I held them in my left hand with my military ID on top and placed my hands at the twelve-o'clock position on the steering wheel.

The night was so still I could hear the locking mechanism disengage as the policeman opened the door of his squad car.

His feet hit the ground, and I listened as the gravel he walked on became louder until he was standing by my driver side door with his flashlight shining in my face preventing me from getting a look at his. At a loss for words, I stared into the light like a deer standing in the middle of the road. Still unable to focus on any identifying features I heard a voice say "boy, what were you doing in Alma?" If you thought I was scared before, now I am almost at the point of panic. I calmly replied "Sir, I am a soldier stationed at Fort Riley and I drove through Alma looking to get gas." In a millisecond I assessed my situation and knew it was best for me to talk slow and keep calm. I felt helpless on this lonely dark highway, and I could feel the potential for things to go left at any moment. During this time in my life, I had served in the military for a few years and knew that feeling of helplessness oh to well, when authority and leadership was abused and weaponized; and this was one of those times. I could no longer stare into the blinding light shining directly in my face, so I turned my head and eyes forward, attempting to prepare myself for whatever was to come next.

"Driver's license, proof of insurance, and registration, please," the officer said.

I extended my left hand out the window with my military ID on top, praying my military service would somehow de-escalate this overwhelmingly passive-aggressive situation. The officer removed the light from my face, and I could hear his footsteps in the gravel on the side of the road as he walked back to his car. Never was silence so loud.

I slightly tilted my head and eyes downward to glance into the driver's-side mirror, ensuring I was extra careful not to make any movements he could interpret as threatening.

I never knew the stillness of the night could be so loud and frightening—almost enough to make you flee, if only for a sense of feeling safe.

The small-town policeman grabbed the microphone to his CB radio, and before he began to speak, I heard the squelch that only a transmitting radio could make.

I was first made aware of that sound as a youngster, growing up with a stepfather who loved nothing more than talking to his buddies on his CB radio.

"I have a name and license plate I need you to run, OVER," the officer said. I sat still and patient, but on the inside, I felt as if I were about to have a myocardial infarction.

What seemed like forever only took a few seconds. The female voice on the other end of the radio came back and said, "He's clean!"

I could have screamed out loud, exited my vehicle, and jumped for joy, but I knew better, so I maintained my posture and sat as still as possible. His door reopened, and I heard his footsteps in the gravel again. The sound grew louder as he got closer to my driver's-side window.

"Here you go—you are good to go," he said as he handed me my credentials. He turned around without another word and walked back to his car.

I placed my driver's license, vehicle registration, proof of insurance, and military ID into the armrest compartment and slowly merged onto the highway after engaging my turn signal.

Thinking this horrible experience was over, I quickly got up to speed and was thrilled to put this behind me.

At a quick glance, I noticed the policeman was following me again. I instantly felt my blood pressure skyrocket, and I could hear my heart beating in my ears once more. Moving slowly, as if the policeman were sitting in the car with me, I reached over and set my cruise control to make sure I would not exceed the speed limit.

After about five miles, the police officer turned on his rotating lights, reduced his speed, and made a U-turn across the grassy median that divided the highway before heading in the opposite direction. I watched his taillights until they disappeared into the darkness of the night.

I drove for another thirty to forty minutes until I came to the crest of what I believed to be a mountain. Down in the valley below sat one of the most beautiful and impressive sights I had ever seen— Marshall Army Airfield. Although I was more than 1,000 miles from the place I grew up, I suddenly felt safe. Marshall Army Airfield sits on the outskirts of Fort Riley, Kansas, and borders I-70, almost geologically centered in the United States.

The airfield was massive, with miles of concrete and more helicopters than I had ever seen in one place at one time. It was quite an impressive display of military firepower, and I drove by in awe.

I made my exit off the highway to be processed through the security post and gladly presented my military ID once again. The gate guard said, "Duty first—welcome to the home of the Big Red One, SGT Payne!" I replied, "Thank you," as I retrieved my ID and slowly drove onto the post, which felt like a safe place for me to be.

CSM Smith and Basic Non-commissioned Officers Course

After in-processing the post, I reported to my unit to begin in-processing into the same unit I had belonged to just a year earlier. Entering the double doors of the battalion headquarters and walking down a highly polished tiled floor, I turned left into the main office. I then stood in front of a long countertop that divided the room from the human-resources personnel and the soldiers who entered the office in need of their services. A loud and familiar voice filled the room: "Payne, you're back!"

It was Command Sergeant Major Smith, the highest enlisted member with whom I had a personal connection from years before.

"Yes, Sergeant Major!" I answered as he approached me with his right hand extended. I reached out my right hand, and we shook hands with what appeared to be mutual respect from two soldiers who had shared some time together.

After exchanging a few pleasantries, he asked, "SGT Payne, are you promotable?"

I answered, "Yes," with so much pride I think my chest stuck out just a bit.

Sergeant Major Smith then said, "Payne, come with me!" I followed him around the counter into the back of the office, where he introduced me to another Sergeant.

Shortly thereafter, he issued a direct order: "Put SGT Payne on the first thing smoking to the Basic Non-Commissioned Officers Course (BNCOC is pronounced *B-knock*)."

The Sergeant replied, "Sergeant Major, SGT Payne is not on my merit list." Without hesitation, Sergeant Major Smith fired back, "Sergeant, I don't give a damn about your merit list! I am only going to repeat myself one more time—put SGT Payne on the first thing smoking to BNCOC, or you will be needing somewhere else to work."

"Roger that, Sergeant Major," he replied.

A few days later, I found myself reporting for duty at Fort Hood, Texas, to begin the Basic Non-Commissioned Officers Course. I did not expect to have the opportunity to attend BNCOC this soon.

However, I was extremely grateful because the course was required for me to achieve my next promotion from Sergeant to Staff Sergeant.

LAND NAVIGATION

A few days after in-processing, I was on the road again driving from Fort Riley, Kansas, to what was then called Fort Hood, Texas—a large Army installation next to a Texas town named Killeen.

I arrived on base with a great deal of optimism and was ready to get started on my road to promotion.

After signing into my temporary duty station, they held a formation for accountability and provided the trainees with a formal introduction to the cadre who would be facilitating our training.

When my name was called, the cadre did not hesitate to mention that Sergeant Major Smith had called ahead to grease the skids.

He shared with the school's leadership that I was one of the sharpest young Cavalry Scouts he had the opportunity to watch grow in our chosen military occupational skill.

The other guys in the course took a moment to rag on me a little before the cadre moved on to the next Sergeant on the list for accountability.

Once the cadre was satisfied with accountability and had provided rules, regulations, and guidelines, one of the Sergeants approached me and said, "So, you are SGT Payne!" He went on to say he had heard much about me after he arrived at our unit in Kansas, shortly after I departed for Korea.

I didn't think much of our encounter, but SGT Hawkins would become a thorn in my side for the next few years. Later in the course, we had our first training exercise quickly approaching.

It is important for soldiers in the Army, sailors in the Navy, airmen in the Air Force, and Marines to maintain a high level of proficiency with their firearms and to qualify at a shooting range periodically throughout the year.

Along with small-arms weapons qualification, a Cavalry Scout is also taught land navigation in basic training.

Before we were allowed to graduate and earn the right to call ourselves soldiers, we had to show proficiency in using a compass to shoot an azimuth, read a map, and create four-digit, six-digit, and eight-digit grid coordinates.

At each level of leadership, it was required that you complete a mandatory professional growth course before becoming eligible for your next promotion.

Just like any other professional leadership development course, land navigation was required to graduate. However, a different twist was added at this level of leadership. We were required to complete a land-navigation course while commanding an M3 Bradley Fighting Vehicle.

M2 Bradley Cavalry Fighting Vehicle

The Bradley Fighting Vehicle, in my opinion, is a very unique and powerful tank in the U.S. Army's arsenal. Its armament consists of a 25-mm main gun with a 900-round capacity, capable of firing either armor-piercing or high-explosive rounds with the click of a button.

In addition to the main gun, the Bradley is armed with two TOW anti-tank missile launchers as well as a 7.62-mm coaxial M-240 Charlie machine gun.

Although the Bradley has a seven-passenger capacity, there are four positions for team operations. The Commander, Gunner, Driver, and Loader make up the four-man team needed to operate the Bradley at optimum proficiency and maximum effectiveness.

During BNCOC, we were required to complete a land-navigation course on one of the largest military installations in the Army's inventory. Several poles with combinations of letters and numbers were placed at different sites to identify locations associated with grid coordinates. From a tactical standpoint, the Army always provided alternative methods to accomplish most tasks. If I had a dollar for every time I heard, "There is more than one way to skin a cat," I would probably be one of the wealthiest men alive today.

Although the military lives on the cutting edge of technology, it was also important for us as leaders to master land navigation without the use of GPS—you never knew when and if technology may fail. I was taught to always be able and prepared to dance on any set when required to do so.

The day came for our class to complete the land-navigation course. When evaluated in all tasks, both hands-on and written examinations we received two status indicators: GO or NO-GO.

If you received a GO status, that meant you had shown yourself proficient at that task and could move on to the next. If you earned a NO-GO, you would receive additional training and be provided a second chance to gain a GO for the previously failed attempt.

In true Army fashion, we woke early for accountability formation and were marched to morning chow—which I learned shortly after retirement is called breakfast. After scarfing down morning chow with the minimum time allowed to eat, the group was formed and marched to the motor pool, where we were assigned a Bradley to command for the duration of the field exercise.

Soon after, we received a safety briefing, loaded our bags, and lined up to leave the comforts of the barracks for the simplicity of outdoor living. Now briefed, loaded, and lined up in a single-file line, we headed out to a designated location where we set up a perimeter, similar to what we would do in a real wartime situation.

We then powered down our vehicles and set up camouflage nets above the Bradley's, simulating the effort necessary to conceal our tank locations from aircraft flying overhead. With no time to spare, the cadre called for us to gather in the center of the tactical circle to determine who would be the first to attempt the land-navigation course.

As we stood there with our Kevlar helmets resting under our armpits, the cadre took one look at me and said, "SGT Payne, since your Sergeant Major has spoken so highly of you, would you mind doing us the honor of showing us how it is done?" Trying not to show my nervousness, I answered, "Hooah, Sergeant!" You are probably wondering what the word *Hooah* means. *Hooah* is a slang term used in the U.S. Army and means "yes" or "understood."

According to *army.mil*, it is believed to have originated from the acronym **HUA**, which stands for "Heard, Understood, and Acknowledged."

However, during my time in the Army, it was the Swiss Army knife of words in our vocabulary—it meant any and everything except *no*.

As I began to secure my helmet, SGT Hawkins spoke out in a very authoritative tone and said, "Let me go first. I am a better Scout than he is!" The cadre turned his head and locked eyes with me, silently asking if I minded. I quickly replied, "Sure!" Relieved that I did not have to go first, I gladly stepped aside and allowed SGT Hawkins the opportunity to demonstrate his claim of being a better Scout than I was.

SGT Hawkins received his instructions, mounted his vehicle, and headed on his way. We all stood around telling war stories to mask our nervous energy as we waited for our turn to navigate the course. A great deal of time passed, and the cadre began to worry.

He picked up the hand mic on his radio and called for SGT Hawkins, but his responses were weak and inaudible.

He tried several times, and after a while, all we could hear was a squelching sound, I was familiar with from my childhood. It became evident to all of us that SGT Hawkins was lost in the woods on one of the largest military installations in the world. Formerly known as Fort Hood, it has a land mass of over 158,000 acres and once had a population of more than 50,000 soldiers.

Because SGT Hawkins had been MIA for such a long period of time and darkness was approaching, a quick assessment of the situation warranted swift action. The cadre changed the radio frequency to call in a helicopter unit that was on standby for situations like this. As he pulled up, everyone was abuzz and couldn't wait to make fun of him for getting lost and becoming a first-time NO-GO at land navigation. The driver moved the tank into its position, and SGT Hawkins made his dismount and started walking toward the group formed in the center of the tactical area.

He knew he was in for it, and the trash-talking started as soon as he headed in our direction. In an effort to minimize some of the damage about to be inflicted upon his already bruised ego, SGT Hawkins repeatedly stated, "I'm humbled, I'm humbled."

In order for us to complete the course, we had to show masterful proficiency in land navigation, both during the day and at night. Because it was now dark and no one had successfully completed the course, the cadre made the decision to start our night land-navigation requirement a day earlier than scheduled.

I then heard, "SGT Payne, do you think you can now show us how it is done?" Like before, I replied, "Hooah, Sergeant!" I secured my gear and received my instructions, along with a set of grid coordinates of points on the ground where poles displayed codes of letters. I was required to record those codes and provide them to the cadre upon my return as proof of my navigational skills.

I headed out to complete the night land-navigation course requirement. I can't remember every point, but I clearly recall standing out of the turret with a map, compass, and night-vision goggles affixed to my face. It was a brisk night, and the sky was so clear I could see every star in space.

What took my peer an entire day to attempt—only to come up empty-handed in daylight—took me just a few hours to accomplish in the dark.

When I returned to the holding area, I turned in my sheet with the identifying letters associated with each point to our instructor, as everyone stood around waiting to see whether I would earn a first-time GO at this station. I noticed SGT Hawkins standing nearby and could almost feel his stare through the moonlit night as the cadre's flashlight glared down onto the paper I had just handed over.

He carefully checked each answer, one by one. Then he looked up and said, "SGT Payne, you are a first-time GO at this station. Good job, Sergeant!" You would have thought I had single-handedly won a war. Sergeants erupted with cheers, jumping around and congratulating me for accomplishing a task we all feared because of the level of difficulty it presented to all of us.

It was as if I had done the impossible. Many of us had a difficult time maintaining our confidence, especially after the debacle we all witnessed earlier that day.

Once the guys saw it could be done, their confidence levels began to trend upward—but not everyone was happy for me that night.

Everyone had an opportunity to navigate the landscape, and everyone completed both the day and night land-navigation exercises. Because of that, we were able to save ourselves from the embarrassment of being dropped from the course and sent back to our units as failures.

SGT Hawkins stayed quiet for a while, licking his wounds from the embarrassment he suffered during land navigation, but his silence wouldn't last long. I imagine he thought that if he said very little, his silence would prevent the other guys from making fun of him—but he was extremely wrong.

Without provocation, someone mentioned him getting lost and so far out of range that he could not be reached by radio—and these were not your standard CB radios.

These are Army-issued PRC-77 radios (pronounced *prick-77*), with a range of five to fifteen miles without an amplifier, depending on the terrain. All it took was for one soldier to mention SGT Hawkins's unfortunate event, and—like sharks aroused by blood in the water—the frenzy would begin all over again. Joke after joke, comment after comment was made until it was almost unbearable to witness.

It was like watching a comedian roast a spectator sitting in the front row of a comedy show until the person finally breaks, stands up, and walks out. However, SGT Hawkins was stuck, with nowhere to go to escape the onslaught of jokes at his expense.

It had gotten so bad that even the course instructors started laughing and joining in on the massacre. I could see his frustration mounting, and he needed a way out—and he needed one fast.

Although I refrained from sharing any of my quick-witted jokes, I couldn't keep myself from laughing along with the rest of the guys. Many of us laughed so hard we physically cried real tears as our stomachs began to hurt from the prolonged comedy roast—and then it all turned left.

Out of nowhere, SGT Hawkins looked in my direction and said, "When we get back to Fort Riley, I am going to get promoted, become your supervisor, and then I am going to get you kicked out of the Army!"

After his abrupt comment, the laughter dissipated like fog lifting after the sun comes up. Quick on my feet, I replied, "When we get back, you are going to do your job—and I am going to do mine."

And just like that, everything returned to normal, as if nothing had ever happened. But that was only the beginning of what SGT Hawkins had in store for me.

Graduation Day finally came. I remember getting up that morning and putting on my Dress Green uniform with all my awards and decorations on my jacket. We called it *full battle rattle*—which is Army jargon that simply meant putting on all your gear or equipment. In this case, it meant putting on all my awards and decorations.

It was a somewhat cold and rainy day, but I was good with it because we would graduate indoors due to inclement weather. The graduation ceremony was a success. We all said our goodbyes and departed Texas just as we had come, heading back to our permanent duty stations across the United States.

CHAPTER THREE
WHO'S LAUGHING NOW?

Meet Your New Supervisor

Still Still floating on cloud nine from the successful completion of BNCOC, I settled into my room in the barracks and prepared for my first day reporting to my assigned platoon. Monday couldn't seem to come fast enough, as I wrestled with the same fear, anxiety, and excitement that many soldiers experience when reporting to a new duty station. However, this time it was different for me. My heightened sense of anxiety came more from meeting new people than from the duty station itself, due to the amount of time I had spent at Fort Riley, Kansas just a year prior.

Monday morning finally came, and it started with the loud, pulsating beeping of my alarm clock, purposely positioned on a small table across the room. This was a strategic move I adopted early in my career to decrease my chances of being late, because I found it difficult to resist the snooze button. The first part of my day was physical fitness, which we called PT.

In the 1990s, we usually had PT every Monday, Wednesday, and Friday at 0600 hours for about an hour or two. These PT sessions were much like the others—just a few minutes of stretching, warm-up exercises, and a two- to five-mile run.

After PT, I took a shower, donned my Battle Dress Uniform (BDU), and headed to the dining facility—or, for those who served, what we referred to as the mess hall—before our 0900 hours accountability formation. After the larger muster, we broke out into smaller groups down to a platoon-size element.

It was then that I met the entire platoon, including my new team leader, Sergeant Frierson. He was a short guy in stature but looked like he spent plenty of extra time in the gym. I was informed that I would be Sergeant Frierson's gunner, and I looked forward to working with him in preparation for our upcoming annual Bradley Table VIII training exercise. This training exercise always separated the boys from the men by spotlighting the Cavalry Scouts who were the best at our craft.

Sergeant Frierson did not hesitate to establish rapport. He asked if I minded eating lunch with him that day so he could share his philosophy and get an opportunity to know me a little better.

During lunch, I could sense his curiosity about my professional efficiency and effectiveness. The majority of our conversation was a test of my knowledge and aptitude as it related to the workings and operation of the M2 Bradley. Although we were the same grade, Sergeant Frierson outranked me by position; however, it quickly became evident that my knowledge on the subject superseded his. He then relaxed and treated me as an equal.

I have never been the type to lower someone else's flag to raise my own, and Sergeant Frierson and I got along great. I was careful not to overstep his authority and carried out my duties to his specifications. Over the course of a few months, we developed a solid friendship, and he began to share some of his more personal thoughts. Many of the things he shared were matters you would only tell someone you felt comfortable with. Sergeant Frierson shared with me that he planned on exiting the Army for civilian life and relocating to his wife's hometown in Europe.

It was important that he held on to that information until the last possible minute due to the possibility of ostracization.

During this era, soldiers felt you were disloyal and abandoning your brothers-in-arms when someone made the decision to trade in their uniform for a chance at civilian life. Before I knew it, Sergeant Frierson had endured cold shoulders and negative feelings from the entire platoon, as well as others from higher levels of command, before slipping into civilian life.

Shortly after the departure of Sergeant Frierson, SGT Hawkins was promoted from Sergeant to Staff Sergeant (SSG). Instead of celebrating his promotion with family and friends, he immediately requested a meeting with our Company Commander and Platoon Sergeant following his promotion ceremony. I could see them from the hallway outside the office through a small, elongated, bullet-proof window with cross-sectioned wires embedded in the glass, standing around the commander's desk in deep discussion, as if they were planning something or making some type of leadership decision.

I instantly began to feel nauseated and sick to my stomach. I could feel the tide changing—and it was not changing in my favor.

I stood outside in the hallway with the rest of the platoon, waiting as if I were an expectant father.

Finally, the door opened, and the newly promoted SSG Hawkins entered the hallway with an evil grin on his face, like a villain from a blockbuster thriller, as he looked me dead in the eyes. Walking directly toward me, he veered slightly to my side, almost grazing my shoulder as he passed by, simultaneously whispering, "I told you so."

The Platoon Sergeant was the next to exit the Commander's office, yelling down the hallway, "1st PLATOON, FORMATION!"

New Crew and Assignments

Formation was mostly held out front of the barracks, in between the parked cars in an oversized parking lot. There we stood, covered-down and dress-right-dressed, with the military precision you would only expect from a highly disciplined and trained unit. "PLATOON, AH-TEN-TION!"

You could hear the heels of every soldier's boot coming together in unison as the platoon snapped to the position of attention. "At ease," said the platoon sergeant before he began disseminating his information.

Clutching a set of index-cards he started sharing his directives as he slowly got around to announcing what would be his daily informational finale. "SGT Payne, you are now the Commander of SSG Hawkins's old track vehicle Alpha-33 (A-33)" and to add insult to injury, he also said "you are also his wingman!" I would later find out that during this time I was the only Sergeant Bradley Commander on the entire installation. However, all of that was overshadowed by the apparent prophecy of SSG Hawkins previously made during our time in BNCOC together several months earlier now has come to fruition. During the following week SSG Hawkins would assign me a crew of his likings. In order for a Bradley crew to perform at its best a team of four men are needed to achieve battle ready proficiency. A Bradley crew consist of a Commander, Gunner, Driver, and Loader. First assigned to me was my gunner.

He was a soldier that until this moment in his army career never served on a M-3 Bradley and would require a great deal of training. Second assigned was my driver although he had some experience as a Bradley crewman, he showed up to work with a cast on his dominate foot. I hope you noticed I did not mention a loader.

To make matters worse, SSG Hawkins failed to assign me one. "He is a super scout—he doesn't need a loader," a throwback comment from our time in BNCOC that came back to haunt me.

Once my team was assembled, I knew what needed to be done if my crew and I were going to make it out of this predicament with our careers intact. I began an intense training regimen with one goal in mind, and that goal was to create extensions of myself. I set out to pour every ounce of knowledge I had acquired over the years into these two soldiers until I had no doubt, they were effective, proficient, and confident in the warrior tasks and drills of a 19 Delta Cavalry Scouts.

Lead By Example

Every day under the leadership of SSG Hawkins presented new challenges. He would go to any length to make me look bad, providing himself opportunities to share my misfortune with our leadership and chip away at my reputation.

One morning after PT and morning chow, SSG Hawkins conducted an impromptu room and equipment inspection. My crew and I were given about a half hour to prepare our barracks rooms, and equipment laid out dress-right-dress for his inspection.

He began his inspection with his soldiers, and the odd thing was that their rooms and equipment were already prepared for inspection before he informed me and my crew. He was up to his same tricks and would pull no punches to set me up for failure. We failed our inspection miserably. Lucky for me, his pop-quiz inspection was only a preview of what was to come.

Later that day, the First Sergeant announced in formation that the company would be having an official inspection in a few days. I had to come up with a plan to pass the next inspection because I could feel the anticipation of the negative counseling statement I was going to receive, along with the snowball effect of the poor performance review SSG Hawkins was itching to add to my official records—potentially preventing me from earning future promotions.

I gathered my soldiers in my room after hours to share my idea with them in hopes of getting their buy-in to what I believed was a solid plan. I felt comfortable with our meeting place because SSG Hawkins was married and lived off the installation, and all my soldiers were within arm's reach of me down the hall in the same building.

Once everyone arrived, we shared our mutual disgust over the unfair treatment we received from our section sergeant and how he rode the borders of the regulations to aid in our daily discomfort. We shared our grievances, and then I shared my plan. Everyone agreed to participate. The next day after work, my soldiers met me at the local Army-Navy store. I supplied each of them with a copy of the equipment inventory sheet, and we bought a second set of equipment to be kept in the trunks of our cars. We agreed it would be used for inspection purposes only. My selling point to them was alleviating the need to clean equipment when we returned from long field exercises.

If you have ever participated in an old-fashioned GI party, then you can understand how powerful and compelling my argument must have been to get two young soldiers to spend their hard-earned money on tactical equipment that is issued to us for free.

The morning of the inspection arrived, and my soldiers and I transported our gear from the parking lot and up two flights of stairs like Army ants. We swapped out our grungy, overused, and under-cleaned equipment for the fresh, semi-new equipment we had purchased just a few days earlier.

Our originally issued equipment was stuffed into duffle bags and replaced the inspection equipment in the trunks of our cars. I went from room to room checking the layout of my soldiers' equipment to ensure everything was laid out correctly for display. Beneath my stone face of seriousness was a smile so large my soul was happy. I knew that this day would not be the day of my demise, and SSG Hawkins would not get a mark in his win column for his efforts to discredit me as a soldier.

The inspection started outside in formation, with every soldier in Class A uniforms wearing all awards and decorations. In the old days, whenever a soldier was dressed in any uniform type and accompanied by all his or her equipment, we called it "full battle rattle." After a series of commands and movements—such as open ranks, eyes right, dress-right-dress, arms downward move, and a few others—we were prepared to have our uniforms inspected.

The leadership moved through each rank-n-file stopping directly in front of every soldier, with SSG Hawkins bringing up the rear and performing his ceremonial duty.

There were no surprises here. My soldiers and I were able to make it past the first phase of our inspection without a single deficiency. The moment of the hour was upon us as we moved into the barracks for the final phase of our inspection, where I was sure SSG Hawkins had placed most of his eggs, hoping he would get the opportunity to call out my shortcomings as a leader in the presence of our leadership.

My room and equipment would be the first to be inspected, and I would accompany the leadership—along with SSG Hawkins—into the rooms of my soldiers. Our last orders were to wait inside our rooms with the doors open, and the leadership would inspect each soldier's room and equipment one at a time.

SSG Hawkins yelled out, "AT EASE!" from outside my door, and I swiftly snapped to the position of parade rest, with my fingers extended and joined, thumbs interlocked, and my hands resting in the small of my back as senior leadership entered my room with SSG Hawkins close behind. The Battalion Sergeant Major didn't waste much time in my room at all.

He picked up a few small pieces of equipment to get a closer look and then threw them down in the general vicinity from where he had removed them, before complimenting me on the cleanliness of both my room and equipment.

He then directed my supervisor to annotate his evaluation on the inspection log before executing his facing movement as only a career military man could, the result of years of marching muscle memory, before exiting my room and entering the hallway. Although it was difficult at times, I made a conscious effort to hide my enthusiasm and never poke the bear, because I was unsure of how far SSG Hawkins would go to ruin my career.

Next up were my soldiers, whom I was sure would receive much more scrutiny than I did. Under most circumstances, if you were a squared-away Non-Commissioned Officer (NCO), you would receive a little more leeway than the lower enlisted members. In keeping with the traditions, customs, and courtesies of the Army of yesteryear, I joined the group of NCOs, leading them to the rooms of my soldiers, stopping short to yell, "AT EASE!", and stepping to the side to allow the leadership team to enter each room.

I then took up the rear, entering the room only after my direct supervisor crossed the threshold. One soldier after the other was inspected, and—just like before—each of them received compliments, ending our portion of the inspection with the Sergeant Major shaking my hand and expressing his pleasure with my ability to lead and train my soldiers.

I could physically see the anger on SSG Hawkins's face. He had this little thing he would do when he was upset—he would grit his teeth very hard, and I would watch his jaw muscles flex as if he were chewing gum. Besides that, he would turn extremely red in the face. Knowing his day didn't go as planned made it extremely difficult for my soldiers and I not to spike the football in the end zone, but I was able to keep them under wraps, and we maintained our professionalism and suppressed our emotions for a later time.

Along with the tremendous leadership challenge of preparing my soldiers for the upcoming Bradley Table VIII, I also had to deal with the daily shenanigans of SSG Hawkins. Not one working day passed without him making every effort to set me up for failure.

Every day was a new adventure, as he started his mornings by informing every member of his team of the daily requirements—except for me and my crew. Lucky for me, I learned at an early age that you can learn a lot indirectly through observation. So, I took on the daily challenge of ascertaining information deliberately withheld from me and disseminating it to my two soldiers.

SSG Hawkins really began to feel himself and stretched every inch of his authority in his new role. The older Non-Commissioned Officers (NCOs) would sit around in the office and drink coffee as they shared their war stories from the conflicts of their day. SSG Hawkins had no problem joining in, although he had very little to offer, having served so little time in comparison to the battle-tested, seasoned war veterans whose company he kept. That did not stop him from hanging out anyway, while his soldiers labored outside executing whatever task he had barked out earlier that day. Each workday began almost identical to the one before it, but this day was shrouded with a heightened level of secrecy.

SSG Hawkins informed me after morning chow to report directly to the motor pool and begin working on my track in preparation for the upcoming war-fighting exercise known as Bradley Table VIII.

After receiving my marching orders, I passed the information on to my crew, and we proceeded to the motor pool after we consumed some good Army chow. When my crew and I arrived at the motor pool, we noticed SSG Hawkins's crew attempting to break track to replace their track pads. A Bradley Fighting Vehicle has 166 rubber and steel blocks we called track pads that fit onto the tracks, and when they are worn down, they must be replaced for the vehicle to steer properly—this is the equivalent of changing tires on a car.

With one glance, I quickly assessed the environment and made a command decision. I ordered my crew to put on their mechanic overalls while I acquired the tools and the 166 track pads we would need to complete our task before the end of the day.

SSG Hawkins barely noticed me as he stood around with the senior NCOs, holding his coffee mug, while the rest of us labored outside in the motor pool.

My secret weapon was leading by example. Instead of intentionally abusing my authority like so many other Sergeants chose to do, I led by a set of rules I had adopted. My leadership style was in direct conflict with many of the leaders I had the misfortune of working for—and many of them were exactly like SSG Hawkins. I swore that I would not lead from a position of privilege whenever I was placed in a leadership role. After gathering what was needed to complete the job, I donned my overalls and joined my soldiers in changing the 166 track pads.

With my help, my crew and I were able to change out the track pads on both sides of our vehicle, sweep our space in the motor pool, move the Bradley to its proper place, and lock it—all before lunchtime. This left a motor pool full of Bradley crewmen with the rest of the duty day to complete changing out their track pads before they could be released for the day. SSG Hawkins observed the distress of his crew struggling to finish what would normally be considered an all-hands-on-deck task, while he maintained his predictable authoritative leadership style and stood by watching his soldiers work, doing nothing to contribute to completing the task.

After lunch, upon returning to the motor pool, SSG Hawkins couldn't believe we had changed our track pads so quickly. My crew and I relished in his embarrassment and the anger he displayed over us finishing our task in what some would call record-breaking time. This day marked the first time I truly tested the strength of my leadership.

Fueled by his anger from our triumphant moment, SSG Hawkins ordered me to have my soldiers assist his soldiers in changing the track pads on his vehicle. There was no way I could allow SSG Hawkins to take advantage of my soldiers—especially after they had worked so hard to complete the same task he had refused to work alongside his own team to finish.

I refused his direct order, and he threatened me with non-judicial punishment under the Uniform Code of Military Justice. I showed him a different side of me that he had never seen until that day. I explained the consequences of his actions and how he was abusing his authority. I all but dared him to move forward with his plans, because we both knew he didn't have a leg to stand on. Still, I also knew this would not be enough to make him stop. It was only a bandage for the time being—and he would not peacefully go away.

CHAPTER FOUR
"The Gun Don't Fit"

The morning my soldiers and I had trained so hard for had finally come. This training exercise was designed to assess the war-fighting capabilities of the crew as a team. It also provided the command with an opportunity to evaluate each crew's ability to identify, engage, and destroy enemy vehicles amid the chaos and pressure of a simulated wartime environment.

Beyond that, the crew that achieved a perfect 1,000-point score would earn the ultimate bragging rights among their peers and gain the respect of senior leadership—both enlisted and officer alike. I swear, the Army has thought of everything.

Every military vehicle came with a book that was the equivalent of an owner's manual on steroids, known as a technical manual, or TM for short. It was mandatory that you learn your vehicle's TM inside and out. After years of performing maintenance checks on our Bradley, much of it became second nature. There was very little you could ask me about my vehicle that I did not already know.

Every so often, we encountered a maintenance issue that required a master mechanic to resolve. When this happened, the vehicle commander would annotate the problem on a maintenance log DA Form 2404, marking it with a circled X to indicate the severity of the issue. A non-rotating turret was exactly the kind of problem that warranted such notation.

I felt on edge going into this gunnery exercise because the previous preventive-maintenance session had uncovered several service issues with my inherited Bradley, some of which were very serious. An unexplained loss of power to the turret nearly sidelined my crew and me. However, just a few days before the field exercise began, the maintenance team was able to restore power to the turret, keeping us in the competition.

Our wait was over, and the day started early—even by military standards.

During this exercise, no expense or effort was spared in creating the most realistic wartime environment possible. Leadership kicked off the event by initiating the alert roster at 0200 hours.

The Battalion Commander alerted the battalion, the battalion alerted the companies, the companies alerted the platoon sergeants, and the process continued until every soldier in the command had been notified.

Each crewmember had a defined set of responsibilities, and because of the repetitive training and rehearsals, everyone moved effortlessly to accomplish their part for the collective mission.

The Army is a stickler for accountability and inventory. Everything—and I mean *everything*—in the Army is accounted for, inventoried, and assigned to someone.

My gunner and I went to the arms room to draw our personal weapons, as well as the weapons assigned to our track vehicle, Alpha-33. As a Bradley Commander, I was issued a .45-caliber handgun and an AR-15 rifle.

With our duffle bags packed full of gear—clothing, toiletries, extra boots, and additional food—we carried the vehicle-assigned weapons down to the motor pool for mounting and integration into the Bradley's automatic firing system.

The entire operation was planned down to the smallest detail, and there was no time to waste. Once our gear was secured, we turned our full attention to uploading the weapons into the Bradley.

The main gun went in first. The receiver of the M-242 25-mm chain gun seated smoothly and without a hitch. However, from the back ramp, I observed my gunner struggling to properly mount the M-240 Charlie machine gun.

Although the M-240 Charlie is not the main gun, the 7.62-mm, belt-fed, gas-operated machine gun is capable of firing 700 to 800 rounds per minute and is a must-have on the battlefield.

Feeling the pressure of the time constraints to line up and roll out of the motor pool in a tactical formation, I walked to the back of the turret and stuck my head inside to ask my gunner what was going on. Yelling over the loud exhaust of a battalion-sized element of Bradley's, he said, "Sarge, it doesn't fit!"

My immediate response was to take his place inside the turret and try it myself. After a few attempts, I too was unsuccessful at mounting the machine gun in its proper place inside the turret.

I sat there for a moment to catch my breath before trying again. After a few additional attempts, I was just about to give up and notify my chain of command of the issue.

Then, out of nowhere, SSG Hawkins appeared on the lowered ramp at the back of my vehicle, yelling at the top of his lungs, "SGT PAYNE BROKE THE 240 CHARLIE!"

He repeated it over and over until he gained the attention of everyone around. I assure you, I am not comparing myself to Jesus, but it felt like he was shouting, *Crucify him!*

Hawkins continued his belligerent behavior until the Sergeant Major came over to investigate what was going on. Even then, Hawkins repeated the accusation again, making sure his message landed. Due to the strict time constraints, the Sergeant Major made a command decision and ordered us to line up for rollout, stating that we would deal with the issue later. My position in the convoy was directly behind SSG Hawkins. As we rolled down the tank trails of Fort Riley, I repeatedly snuck down into the turret, making attempt after attempt to mount the machine gun. No matter how much I tried, it would not fit into the mounting brackets.

The Set-up Secured

After what felt like an entire day of riding tank trails through the forest, we finally arrived at the range where our glorified weapons qualification would take place. We positioned the vehicles side by side in a gravel parking lot and unloaded all of our gear onto the back of a 2½-ton truck for transport to the temporary barracks facility where we would be living for the next week or so. I made every attempt to remain upbeat and positive. However, I could feel the mist from a dark cloud following me. In that moment, I understood how SSG Hawkins must have felt after the embarrassment he suffered during BNCOC. Although I had not joined the dog pile when the jokes were being told, I knew I would feel the full wrath of his revenge.

He would not let up. SGT Hawkins told every soldier within arm's length that SGT Payne had damaged his M-240 Charlie machine gun.

As the saying goes, it is no fun when the rabbit has the gun. As we settled into our temporary facility, the feeling of ostracization began to set in. There was no escaping the stares or the whispers throughout the compound.

My usual peer group avoided me like the plague, which caused me to stick closer to my soldiers. Although they were subordinate to me, they were the only group with whom I felt comfortable and safe.

I started feeling like a fugitive on borrowed time—as if the Feds were closing in and it was only a matter of time before everything came crashing down. It didn't take long for my intuition to prove correct.

The very next morning, while I was sitting in the dining facility, SSG Hawkins entered the chow hall like a prehistoric dinosaur hunting prey. He stood just beyond the threshold of the entrance and scanned the room, and my gut told me he was searching for me.

I watched his head rotate on his neck as if it were computer-engineered, pausing briefly as his focus shifted from one table to another. It wasn't long before our eyes locked. A smirk appeared on his face as he began walking in my direction.

I knew this would be the beginning of a very bad day.

"SGT Payne, you need to report to the Company Commander and the First Sergeant, ASAP!"

With my breakfast half eaten, I stood to my feet, discarded my plate, and departed the mess hall for what I knew would be bad news. I had learned that bravery and fear appear identical to the naked eye, and I walked at a self-assured pace toward what I was certain would be my doom.

I entered a nearly unfinished, open-bay barracks-style room filled with multiple rows of metal bunk beds—designed for numbers, not comfort. Through the openings between the top and bottom bunks, I could see a group of soldiers congregating in the rear of the bay, and instinctively, I knew they were there for me.

With my fear disguised as bravery, I confidently walked to the back of the room to face whatever was in store. As I made my approach, I stopped short, snapped to the position of attention, and rendered the proper military customs and courtesies.

"At ease, SGT," the Company Commander (CO) ordered, before beginning to outline the course of action he intended to take regarding the damage to an expensive piece of military armament.

The Company Commander informed me that I would be issued a new machine gun to participate in the field exercise.

Without missing a beat, he also told me that I was under investigation and then introduced me to the investigating officer.

It felt as if the weight of the world was crushing me, yet no one seemed to notice. To add insult to injury, no one appeared to care.

I was preparing to begin a weapons qualification with a tank, an inexperienced crew, and a Bradley plagued with maintenance issues. As if that weren't enough, I was now under investigation for a bent machine gun made of steel. I can't tell you how I managed to persevere and not throw in the towel, but I kept moving forward as if it were truly mind over matter.

It appeared that SSG Hawkins had the whole world in the palm of his hand—at least our world. He ordered me to report to his buddy in the arms room to turn in the broken machine gun and sign for a loaner to be used for the remainder of the training exercise.

I gathered my soldiers and briefed them on the details and seriousness of the investigation I was under. Because of the weight of the machine gun, I enlisted their help to carry the damaged weapon to the arms room. After I took responsibility for it, we returned to the Bradley and uploaded the loaner machine gun into its proper place.

Once the weapon was mounted, my team and I conducted pre-fire checks one last time in preparation for receiving live ammunition and beginning our live-fire exercise the following day.

The Perfect Score

The next morning came quickly as the alarm on my digital watch went off in my ear. I had fallen asleep in the fetal position with my head resting in my left hand. My feet hit the floor simultaneously as I reached under the head of my bunk to grab my toiletry bag and slid my feet into my shower shoes.

I seemed to stand up in sections until I was fully upright, finishing my movements with a stretch and a yawn—putting the cherry on top of a good night of deep REM sleep. With my toiletry bag in hand, I walked out of the barracks and down the street to the latrine, making my way to the closest available sink not in use.

After my hygienic morning ritual, I gathered my toiletry bag, walked back to the barracks, and dressed for the activities of the day. The entire unit was upbeat and anxious to start firing live ammunition at the presented targets for points and the chance to call themselves the Top Gun.

During live-fire exercises, every soldier assigned a position on a Bradley wore an olive-drab flight suit. The Army has a way of boosting your ego with simple things—ribbons, medals, and uniforms.

This day would prove to be one filled with adventure and infinite possibilities.

My soldiers and I walked to the mess hall to secure a table so we could sit together and eat our morning chow: scrambled eggs, hash browns covered with sausage gravy, two slices of bacon, and white toast—buttered and cut diagonally from the top left corner to the bottom right.

After breakfast, we gathered our gear and assembled at the designated pickup point to be transported to the range for our Day One safety briefing and to sign for the ammunition needed to complete the course.

The Day One safety briefing was long, and the Master Gunner spelled out every detail of the do's and don'ts once we occupied the range with live ammunition.

I swear to you, the Army has thought of everything.

To keep the qualification competition fair, each Bradley commander signed for the exact amount of ammunition required. If you expended too many rounds on one target, you risked running out of ammunition toward the end of the exercise—potentially costing you and your crew the opportunity to earn the coveted 1,000-point score and all the bragging rights that came with it.

In the midst of all the drama, the mechanics fixed my tank, and my crew and I were able to upload our ammunition and prepare for the first day of competition.

SSG Hawkins and his crew had the honor of engaging the targets first, while my crew and I waited in the staging area for their return. They came back after firing their first group of targets and immediately received their debriefing. The Army made a big deal out of this entire process.

After each crew engaged a set of targets, they would dismount their tank and receive a detailed debrief from a group of Sergeants with specialized training, tasked with evaluating every nuance of battle precision demonstrated by the tank crew.

SSG Hawkins and his crew departed the debriefing happier than I had ever seen them in the years I had worked with them.

He couldn't wait to let me know that he and his crew had achieved a perfect first run of 200 points and that he was going to score 1,000 points to prove he was a much better Cavalry Scout than I was. After listening to him gloat over his early success, it was finally my crew's turn to go downrange and see how we measured up against SSG Hawkins and his crew's initial engagement.

My crew and I moved to the starting point and waited for instructions from the tower.

"Alpha-Three-Three, this is the tower, OVER!"
"Tower, this is Alpha-Three-Three, OVER!"

"Enemy tanks have been spotted in your vicinity. Move out and scan your lane."

I gave my driver the go-ahead to proceed down the tank trail at a slow speed. We were fully buttoned up inside the Bradley with our hatches closed, communicating through the intercom systems connected to our helmets while scanning the terrain through night-vision periscopes.

Our first target popped up, and I issued the precision fire command to my crew, granting my gunner authorization to engage our very first target using live ammunition.

"Gunner, PC, one-two-hundred, HE, FIRE!"

I know that sounds like a bunch of jibber-jabber, but it's actually quite simple once you understand it.

The first part of the command alerts the gunner to prepare to engage a target. The next part of the fire command tells the crew—primarily the gunner—what he will be shooting at; PC stands for *Personnel Carrier*. The final elements of the command provide the distance in meters (1,200), the ammunition type (high explosive), and my authorization as the commander to fire at the target, as well as when to stop firing—*cease fire*.

Our first set of target engagements included both a gunner's engagement and a commander's engagement. So far, everything was going well. My gunner responded perfectly to the hours of training he had received, and now it was my turn to match SSG Hawkins and his crew with 200 points for the first day of shooting.

"Alpha-Three-Three, this is the tower, OVER."

"Tower, this is Alpha-Three-Three, OVER."

"An enemy vehicle has been spotted in your vicinity. Your gunner's controls are no longer working. You will have to engage the target from the commander's controls. Good luck and scan your lane. OVER."

"Move out, driver."

As the driver began moving slowly down the tank trail, the target meant for me to engage popped up—and suddenly my turret lost power. I immediately ordered the driver to stop and notified the tower of my vehicle malfunction.

A few words were exchanged, and the decision was made to bring in the maintenance tank, the M-88, to tow my crew and me off the range so other crews could continue engaging targets that day.

As the maintenance crew worked to connect the tow bar to my vehicle, I spoke without thinking, joking over the radio frequency shared by the other soldiers listening in.

"Wouldn't it be something if I shot my target manually while being towed down the range?"

A few servicemembers broke squelch, keyed their microphones, and laughed over the airwaves. Then a voice of distinction came across the radio and said, "This is SIX. Let's do it!"

He continued, "If you miss the target, we will alibi you, and when your tank is fixed, you'll get another chance to engage your target."

If you don't know, SIX is a Battalion Commander. He oversees millions of dollars' worth of Army inventory and commands a thousand or more soldiers. I was glad he said he would alibi my attempt because it was definitely a check I knew I could not cash. In that moment, I realized I had stuck my foot deep into my mouth.

The maintenance crew finished connecting the tow bar and switched their radio to my frequency.

We both buttoned our hatches, received our scenario from the tower, and I issued my command—not to my own driver, but to the maintenance driver. "Driver, move out."

The maintenance vehicle slowly began pulling my broken tank down the tank trail as the target popped up, moving swiftly from left to right.

The moment I saw it, I yelled my precision fire command into my boom mic to ensure every word could be heard clearly and understood.

"Gunner, PC, one-two-hundred, HE, from my position, FIRE!"

Something happened in that moment that I am certain I could not duplicate again—even if I had a million years to try. Because of the loss of power to my turret, I was forced to use the manual controls, which elevated the level of difficulty to nearly impossible.

Honestly, this was almost biblical.

I'm talking the equivalent of David and Goliath.

Imagine sitting in the turret of a tank with no power, gripping a handle in each hand. The handle in your left hand controlled the elevation of the 25-mm main gun—moving the barrel up and down. The handle in your right hand traversed the turret from left to right. To align my sight on the target, I had to turn both handles simultaneously, clockwise and counterclockwise, while the tank bounced along the trail under tow.

And did I mention that all of this had to be executed while the tank was bouncing up and down as it was slowly being towed along a bumpy tank trail?

Here's the craziest part: the trigger is a button strategically located on the inner, upper portion of the right handle, and you have to depress it with your thumb to fire rounds at the target.

Then the most incredible thing happened.

I hit the target center mass—a feat I knew I would never duplicate again in my lifetime.

The mechanics continued towing my crew and me to the base of the tower, where the Battalion Commander and a host of other soldiers, including a few Vietnam-era veterans, were gathered to greet us. My crew and I unbuttoned our hatches to loud cheers as we dismounted our broken vehicle as if we had saved the world. SIX was ecstatic. What started as a handshake turned into a hug. The Battalion Commander gave my crew and me his custom-made challenge coin, which was reserved for only the most memorable events and the soldiers he chose to bestow what we all believed to be one of the highest honors in the unit.

After the surge of energy died down a bit, we made our way into the building beneath the control tower for debriefing. The debriefing was extremely crowded and very brief.

No one—including the scorers—could overlook what we had all witnessed, and everyone acknowledged that my manual shooting was nothing short of a miracle. Somewhere between successfully engaging my target, receiving the Battalion Commander's challenge coin, participating in a packed debriefing, and matching SSG Hawkins's score, I almost forgot about the investigation into the broken machine gun.

Almost.

It was always in the back of my mind, but I pushed onward as if it didn't exist.

After all the hoopla was over, my crew and I had to remove our ammunition from our tank before it was transferred to the maintenance bay for troubleshooting. Just as I started to let my guard down and relax, the investigating officer reappeared for a second round of questioning.

The investigating officer was an aviation officer who had never had the opportunity to sit in the turret of an M2 Bradley, but that was about to change. He had several questions based on the theories he had developed, speculating how a nearly 28-pound steel machine gun could have been bent in the manner my assigned weapon was. The investigator and I took a short ride to the maintenance area where my Bradley was being held.

Parked next to several other inoperative tanks, the investigating officer assisted me in removing the olive-drab tarp that was secured by ropes attached to the four corners of the vehicle. Using the foot hook on the driver's side, I climbed up onto the cold, mostly hard metal and unlocked the military-grade padlock securing the driver's hatch.

Because the vehicle had no power, I climbed through a narrow space behind the driver's seat, past the outer shell of the turret, and into the rear of the Bradley. From there, I entered the turret and opened both the gunner's and commander's hatches from the inside.

The investigator climbed up onto the turret, passed the main gun barrel, and down into the turret to sit in the commander's seat.

As we sat there, he shared one theory he was wrestling with. He theorized that the machine gun had been left hanging out of the turret and was bent as the turret was turned in one direction or another.

I quickly reminded him that my turret had been broken and without power for the majority of the time I was assigned the vehicle. It had only been fixed a few days before the field exercise—during a timeframe when all of the unit's machine guns were secured in the arms room.

We sat in the turret a little while longer as he ran through several different scenarios of how I could have broken my assigned weapon.

The investigator and I indulged ourselves in a game of mental chess. As soon as he presented a theory, I discredited it. One by one, his explanations fell apart. After a while, the investigator appeared to have exhausted most of his theories, and we sat in the cold silence of the turret.

The Army has thought of everything. During basic training, soldiers are required to learn a host of different hand-and-arm signals and the meanings of various colored flags.

Strategically placed inside the turret was a set of three flags used as a visual communication method with other members of the unit, or as a ground-guide signal for tanks operating in loud, congested environments when verbal communication would be ineffective.

The flag set consisted of three 17-by-16-inch flags—red, green, and orange—with poles approximately 36 inches long and about the girth of a wooden broomstick.

I could tell the investigating officer was really into fitness. He had the physique of a bodybuilder, and it was obvious that he worked out regularly, if not every day.

"So, sir, do you like to work out?" I asked.

"Absolutely!" the young Army captain replied.

"Sir, can you bench-press 200 pounds?"

"Of course!" he answered, as if I had insulted him with the question.

I then asked if he would crank the right handle positioned next to his right knee counterclockwise to traverse the turret left until the rear opening was almost closed.

I grabbed my flag set and placed it on the floor of the turret, allowing half the length of the pole to hang outside of the turret.

I asked the investigating officer to try to break the wooden, broomstick-like flagpole by cranking the turret and closing it on the stick. Once the turret closed onto the flagpole, he cranked as hard as he could. I could see veins bulging from his forehead near his temporal lobe as he began to break a sweat.

Checkmate.

I knew at that moment my position was substantiated—or at the very least, that I had created reasonable doubt.

The investigating officer conceded and stated, "SSG Payne, there is no way you could have bent that machine gun." He was convinced that I did not damage my assigned weapon, although we were both baffled and had no idea how it ended up bent.

The next morning came early, and once again I had to set my worries aside and concentrate on the task at hand—shooting a 1,000-point gunnery.

As if the investigation and an inoperative tank weren't enough, I was informed that my crew and I would have to complete the remainder of our engagements using the tanks of other commanders in the platoon whenever one became available.

This meant that the crew of the tank we borrowed would have to remove all of their ammunition. We would then upload the ammunition I had signed for into that tank's gun system to engage our targets, and once we were finished, we would have to download any remaining ammunition—every single time.

My crew and I bounced from tank to tank until we found ourselves one engagement away from a perfect 1,000-point score.

Of the 50 to 60 tanks assigned to the battalion, only two crews were still in the running for a perfect score. Yep, you guessed it—SSG Hawkins's crew and my crew were neck and neck for the bragging rights that year. It appeared that all our jumping from tank to tank had paid off.

SSG Hawkins and I were tied at 800 points each, and the final set of targets was worth 100 points.

The first target was a gunner's engagement, and the last target within the engagement group was the Bradley Commander engagement from the defilade position.

Just like déjà vu—reminiscent of our time together earlier that year in the Basic Non-Commissioned Officers Course—SSG Hawkins insisted on going ahead of me. He wanted to prove he was the better Cavalry Scout by shooting a perfect score before I had the chance. Hawkins and his crew headed downrange with hopes of becoming the first crew to shoot 1,000 points. Instead of returning from the tank trails with the anticipated joy and excitement, Hawkins dismounted his tank angrier than I had ever seen him.

Once the ramp lowered, I could hear him cursing at his gunner over the loud exhaust of the tank. He slammed his helmet onto the ground, much like a professional football player throwing his helmet to the turf on the sideline after a poorly executed play costs the team a Super Bowl win.

His gunner had missed the target—costing them the 100 points they needed for a perfect score.

SSG Hawkins and his crew filed into the debriefing room beneath the control tower with their heads down, single file, in anticipation of hearing the inevitable news—that they had fallen short of a perfect score. Ironically, that failure had provided SSG Hawkins with what he desired most: an opportunity to humiliate me in the presence of the entire unit.

SSG Hawkins and his crew filed out of the debriefing room just as they had entered, one behind the other, following their unethical leader like a family of Canadian geese trailing a gander to the nearest pond after emerging from the cover of the woods at first light.

The Army, by design, moves on to the next objective quickly, and there was no time to cry over missed targets. Almost instantly, the attention that SSG Hawkins and his crew had been receiving shifted to me and my crew—without a moment's notice—because we were the last opportunity for any crew participating in the gunnery exercise to possibly shoot the nearly impossible 1,000 points.

Our platoon sergeant jumped into action and made the decision for my crew and me to shoot our final two engagements using SSG Hawkins's tank.

When Hawkins caught wind of what was happening, he quickly alerted his crew to grab their belongings, locked his tank, and jumped onto the back of a 2½-ton truck to catch a ride to the barracks containment area.

The platoon sergeant then requested the use of the First Sergeant's Humvee, and we sped off down a tank trail, kicking up a cloud of dust behind us like a train moving across the flat plains of the Midwest.

We found SSG Hawkins in the barracks lying in his bunk. In the short time it took us to track him down, he had already changed out of his uniform and into his physical-fitness sweats and shower shoes. We rushed through the door with my platoon sergeant leading the way.

"SARGE, I need the key to your Bradley! Payne has an opportunity to get a thousand points!"

SSG Hawkins continued lying on his bunk, refusing to make eye contact with either of us. Finally, he spoke.

"NO, he is not using my track!"

Our platoon sergeant appeared shocked at what he was witnessing and offered an explanation to reinforce why I needed to use Hawkins's tank to shoot my final two engagements. SSG Hawkins, however, could not have cared less.

"SSG Hawkins! Give SGT Payne the keys to your track!"

Again, SSG Hawkins answered, "NO!"

I stood there in silence, anticipating how our platoon sergeant would insert his authority with his friend in response to the open defiance and blatant disrespect. He tried again.

"SSG Hawkins, give SGT Payne the keys to your vehicle!"

After a few seconds, SSG Hawkins sat up in his bunk with the keys to his tank in his right hand, his elbows resting on his thighs. He took in a deep sigh and threw the keys—attached to a metal dog tag indented with his vehicle number—onto the concrete floor at my feet.

Sometimes when I think about it, I can still hear the sound those keys made when they hit the floor. As the keys lay at my feet, I raised my head—maintaining my silence—and locked eyes with my platoon sergeant as if to ask, *what are you going to do about this?*

I could physically see the burden on him. He was being forced to chastise a friend with whom he had spent many off-duty hours, simply because his position required it.

He stood a little taller, inhaled deeply, and barked at his friend, "SSG Hawkins, pick up those keys and place them in SGT Payne's hand!"

SSG Hawkins moved slowly. Still bent at the waist, he lifted himself off the mattress and picked up the keys from the floor. Almost at a crawl, he reached down in a four-point stance, using his fingertips to guide the keys into the palm of his right hand before slowly standing to his feet.

As he stood directly in front of me, he was met with my right palm facing upward, waiting to receive the keys.

With a slight smirk of victory on my face, I knew how much he hated placing the keys to his Bradley in my hand. Most of all, he would never be able to live with the fact that I was about to shoot a perfect 1,000-point gunnery using *his* vehicle—given our long history of unhealthy competition.

After he placed the keys in my hand, the three of us stood there in a dark, quiet, empty barracks room lined with rows upon rows of vacant bunk beds. SSG Hawkins and I stood toe-to-toe, while our platoon sergeant positioned himself slightly to my right—centered between us both.

What felt like a few minutes was only a few seconds, but we stood there as if we were in the middle of the squared circle, receiving our instructions before returning to our corners to start round one. I could see the hatred he had for me, but I dared not look away—not even a blink would have served my manhood well.

Out of the tension of the awkward silence, our platoon sergeant finally spoke.

"Come on, SGT Payne—let's go."

The three of us turned and walked away simultaneously, but I managed to get to the door first and didn't stop until I planted myself in the passenger seat of the Humvee.

Seconds behind me, my platoon sergeant slid behind the steering wheel and drove us back to the firing range.

Just as before, we left a trail of dust behind us, flowing in the opposite direction from where we had come.

We reached the base of the tower in record-breaking time, jumping out of the Humvee to prepare SSG Hawkins's Bradley for my crew and me to engage our final two targets—an opportunity to accomplish what no one else had that year: a 1,000-point score at a Bradley Table VIII Gunnery.

My crew and I worked diligently to upload the ammunition I had signed for into SSG Hawkins's Bradley, calming our nerves as we prepared to go downrange and engage our last two targets. We completed all our preliminary checks, received our safety briefing, and lined up at the edge of the firing range just as an aircraft would stage before entering the runway.

After a brief wait, my crew and I received permission from the control tower to enter the firing range. Sitting at the designated starting point, an unfamiliar voice came over the radio and into the speakers in our aviation-style helmets.

"Alpha-Three-Three, you are now cleared to enter the range."

I gave the order for my driver to advance slowly down the tank trail as we scanned our field of fire, looking for the first target to engage. My gunner worked his controls, scanning horizontally back and forth, while I practiced patience—resisting the urge to take control of the system from the commander's panel on my side of the turret.

On the second pass through the field of fire, I spotted a moving target and quickly issued my precision fire commands.

"GUNNER, PC, SABOT, ONE-TWO-HUNDRED, FIRE!"
"Target, Target, Target—Cease Fire!"

My gunnery executed just as we had practiced. After receiving my fire command, my gunner selected the correct ammunition type—armor-piercing rounds, rather than the high-explosive ammunition we carried for a different target set. He then fired a single round, known as a sensing round.

A sensing round tells the crew whether we are on target, and his sensing round was spot on. I gave the order for him to continue firing in three-round bursts for a total of seven hits—one more than the required six needed to receive a *GO* for our first target, symbolic of a kill on the battlefield.

One target down and well on our way to a perfect score, I gave my driver the command to continue moving slowly down the tank trail.

Scanning for our second and final target came with a different kind of pressure—everything was riding on my ability to engage the target from the commander's position. All I had to do was identify the target in time, give the correct fire command, engage, and hit it. If we succeeded, we would be the only crew on the entire installation that year to score a perfect 1,000-point gunnery with a Sergeant E-5 Bradley Commander.

The target popped up, and it was moving fast. Without thinking, my muscle memory kicked in from the countless times I had executed this action before.

SGT Payne and his 1,000 Point Crew

"Gunner, PC, SABOT, One-Two-Hundred, From My Position, FIRE!" "Target, Target, Target—Cease Fire!"

Once the sequence of events was over, I knew we had done it. My crew had been hand-picked by SSG Hawkins to put me at a disadvantage, but somehow, we were on the verge of being crowned the best Bradley Fighting Vehicle crew in the unit.

After I successfully engaged my target, we made our way to the debriefing room to make it official.

You cannot imagine the level of pride we felt that day as we dismounted SSG Hawkins's Bradley.

Although I had participated in 1,000-point crews in the past, I had never done so as a Bradley Commander—and this one felt more special than all the others.

The evaluator took his time going over every single detail of our target sequence before telling us what we were waiting to hear.

"Let me be the first to tell you—congratulations on a perfect thousand-point gunnery!"

My crew and I jumped around in a circle, hugging each other like we had just won a new car on a game show.

The entire leadership team was in attendance to hear the good news, and everyone was over-the-top happy for us—with the exception of SSG Hawkins, of course. My crew and I returned to the tank, downloaded our remaining ammunition, and locked SSG Hawkins's vehicle.

I then placed the keys in my platoon sergeant's hand, and we rode back to the barracks area on the back of a 2½-ton truck used to transport soldiers back and forth from the range.

The entire compound was abuzz, and the news had traveled fast. Everyone in the unit was seeking me out as if I were the newly appointed godfather of a corrupt crime family.

The celebration would be short-lived, as I was quickly brought back to earth when a senior servicemember requested my attention. He asked me to report to the maintenance bay in the motor pool after dinner chow. He stated that he had some valuable information he wished to share with me concerning my investigation. Leaving me very little choice—because he outranked me—I obliged.

I sat with my crew in the mess hall, pretending to be excited during our celebratory dinner as we entertained the other soldiers who gathered around to hear our war stories. However, the anticipation of meeting with one of the senior leaders in the unit had doused what little flame of celebration I had left. The weight of the pending investigation hung over me, and worry about my fate began to set in.

I rushed through my meal and beelined to the motor pool, walking into the office in the back of the maintenance bay, bracing myself for the vital information the senior warrant officer felt compelled to share.

He wasted no time getting straight to the point. What began as an information session quickly transitioned into a confession and ended with him asking for my forgiveness.

As I sat with my arms resting on the armrests of an office chair, I was told a story filled with deceit at a level I had never witnessed before that day. The story would have been unbelievable had I not been the intended recipient of the misfortune that accompanied this web of diabolical coordination.

Approximately a year prior to my return to Fort Riley, Kansas, SSG Hawkins had damaged the very machine gun I was currently assigned and under investigation for.

His friendship with the armorer gave him an opportunity to hide the broken weapon by swapping it out with another, buying himself time until he could devise a plan.

The moment he faced humiliation after getting lost during our land-navigation evaluation in BNCOC, he set a trap in motion—one fueled by the hatred and envy he had stored up just for me. After our graduation from the Basic Non-Commissioned Officers Course, SSG Hawkins was promoted just as he had said he would be.

Armed with the knowledge that he would remain in the same platoon, he was elevated from team leader to section sergeant, which meant he would inherit a different Bradley Fighting Vehicle. His lobbying for me to become his wingman ensured that I would inherit his previous Bradley, Alpha-33 (A-33).

Once he sold the idea of me becoming his team lead and wingman, he set his entire plot into motion—covering up the damage to the machine gun while simultaneously placing me squarely in the crosshairs for the slaughter.

I cannot, for the life of me, figure out what compelled the senior chief warrant officer to share this information with me. Still, I was relieved—and I have never fully expressed my gratitude to him, at least not to the degree he deserved.

I was once told that acid does more damage to the object it is poured on than to the container it is stored in. His confession was overwhelming and filled me with anger and rage—so much so that I felt as though I might explode from the toxicity of the information.

I sat in shock, contemplating what my next move should be. Honestly, I had no idea.

If I ran out and told anyone, it would turn into my word against his, and under the current circumstances, I was certain I would not be able to sway anyone's opinion.

I did not have to ponder long about my next move. The senior chief warrant officer stated that he would do whatever he had to do to clear my name and volunteered to share what he knew about the entire situation with the investigating officer. We shook hands, and I walked away half-skeptical but with a partial sense of vindication.

The next morning came just like the one before it; however, there was something different in the air. I walked to the open-bay locker room to take a shower and brush my teeth to get my day started. With my damp towel draped over my shoulder and my toiletry bag in my left hand, I walked back to the barracks as the sun peeked over the Midwestern horizon to get dressed for morning chow.

As I sat on my bunk lacing up my boots in preparation to join my crew in the dining facility, my platoon sergeant walked over and helped himself to a seat at the foot of my bunk.

"Sergeant, the Battalion Commander would like to speak to you after you finish eating chow."

I asked what it was about, but he offered no additional information. I agreed, continued lacing up my boots, and headed out the door to the chow hall.

Breakfast was awful. I couldn't enjoy my meal while wondering what the Battalion Commander could possibly want to talk to me about. I stood up from the table with a half-eaten plate of food, a gut full of butterflies, and a ton of nervous energy.

I discarded the uneaten food into the trash, passed my tray through the opening in the wall to a soldier on the other side, and headed out the door to report to the Battalion Commander.

Although there was no indication that I was in any immediate trouble or danger, it did nothing to calm my nerves. I was so anxious I could feel my heart in my throat, as if I hadn't chewed my food properly.

I entered the main barracks building occupied by the Battalion Commander and was met by a lineup of who's-who standing around as if they had all been waiting for my arrival.

The room seemed to grow quieter the moment I crossed the threshold, and a path opened—cleared like a runway—leading directly to the Battalion Commander's office.

Without giving any indication of my true feelings, I stood tall with my shoulders squared and my head held higher than ever before. Let's not forget—I was only one day removed from scoring a perfect 1,000 points at our gunnery exercise.

With three firm wraps on the door, I heard a voice of authority say, "ENTER."

And that I did. I turned the doorknob clockwise until the latch sank deep behind the faceplate and would not turn any farther. I pulled the door open and stepped inside, turning my back to those in the room as I twisted the knob on the opposite side until I felt the locking mechanism engage in the palm of my hand. I pulled the door closed firmly, without making a sound.

While holding the door shut with my right hand, I simultaneously twisted the knob counterclockwise, releasing the latch and allowing it to slide freely past the strike plate until the door was fully secured.

Slightly bent at the waist, with the military precision of a soldier in the Old Guard, I walked directly toward the commander, stopping short about two feet from the edge of his desk. I then came to the position of attention and executed a right-face. This placed me centered on the Battalion Commander's desk as I rendered my salute and said, "SGT Payne reporting, Sir!"

"At ease, Sergeant," the Battalion Commander said.

His next request was shocking and caught me completely off guard. He asked me to take a seat and relax. This was highly unusual interaction between a Sergeant (E-5)—or what the old-timers would call a *Buck Sergeant*—and a Lieutenant Colonel (O-5) in the 1990s U.S. Army.

He began the conversation by congratulating me on an outstanding job training my men and becoming the only crew to shoot a perfect 1,000-point gunnery during that year's field exercise.

In his tenure, he stated, he had never seen anything like the display of war-fighting capability my crew and I had demonstrated over the previous few days.

After the pleasantries were offered, he shifted gears and changed the topic of conversation to my pending investigation.

Apparently, a little bird had shared some information about a Sergeant bending a machine gun almost a year to the day at the previous annual Bradley Table VIII field exercise—when I was in the Federal Republic of Korea.

His next statements completely lifted the burden I had carried throughout the entire field exercise, beginning the moment we rolled out of the motor pool while SSG Hawkins stood at the back of my Bradley yelling at the top of his lungs, trying to convince anyone who would listen that I had bent the machine gun he was pinning on me.

The Battalion Commander went on to explain that he was fully aware of the ins and outs of my investigation, and he could say with absolute certainty that I would soon be vindicated, with all charges found to be unsubstantiated.

It felt as if the weight of the world had been lifted off my shoulders and washed away like dirty water flowing down a shower drain.

As swiftly as he had shifted the conversation earlier, he transitioned once again—doubling back to the gunnery results and explaining how he intended to reward my crew and me for a job well done.

There are a few sayings I heard throughout most of my childhood, but I had never seen them in action as clearly as I did on this day.

The first of several actions the Battalion Commander took was astonishing. SSG Hawkins and his crew were responsible for towing my broken tank back to the installation and washing it once they returned. To a civilian who has never had the unfortunate pleasure of spending a day at an Army wash rack, it would be difficult to accurately describe just how miserable that task is. Trust me—this activity should be listed right up there with capital punishment, or at least that's what it always felt like to me. I hope the irony of this isn't lost on you.

The very vehicle SSG Hawkins had been assigned the previous year—when he bent the machine gun—was once again associated with him.

Only this time, it became a shackle created from the failed plan he believed was ironclad in its purpose to ruin my Army career. In addition to towing and washing my tank, SSG Hawkins and his entire crew were also placed on dunnage detail.

This was another one of those degrading Army rituals that always gave me pause about my decision to join the military in the first place. It was like walking at double-arm intervals and picking up cigarette butts when you didn't even smoke.

Except this time, you would find yourself walking an old, graveled tank trail, picking up expended brass shell casings from the hundreds of thousands of rounds fired from tanks over the previous few days.

I felt like I had hit the lottery.

My crew and I were exempt from both the wash-rack duty and dunnage detail. Even more, we were granted an unauthorized five-day pass—something so rare that in my 20 years and 16 days of service, I had never seen or heard of it happening again. Under normal circumstances, soldiers might receive three- or four-day passes, usually tied to a weekend—Friday through Sunday or Friday through Monday.

This time, however, we received five consecutive days off, starting on a Friday and not returning to work until the following Wednesday.

This alone would have been more than enough; however, the Battalion Commander's bag of gifts was not empty, and he reached into it once more.

In a Cavalry unit, the Battalion Commander is transported by several modes of transportation, such as a Humvee and a Bell UH-1 helicopter, which gained its popularity during the Vietnam War—along with its nickname, the *Huey*. His final surprise was beyond a bucket-list item for me, because I was incapable of even dreaming that big.

Yep—my crew and I would receive a ride back to the installation in the Battalion Commander's helicopter.

I could not wait to go back and tell my crew all the good news about what was getting ready to happen.

Once I was free to leave the Battalion Commander's presence, I stood to my feet, snapped to the position of attention, rendered my salute prouder than I ever had before, executed the proper facing movements, and exited the room just as I had entered it.

It took everything in me not to take off into a full sprint to share the news with my crew. I could not differentiate between my personal happiness and my joy for their recognition and acknowledgment for the hard work it had taken for us to get there.

In short order, due to the limited amount of time I had to inform my crew of what was about to happen, I settled on giving them both direct orders to grab their belongings and meet me outside the barracks. In true soldier fashion, neither of them questioned my request. Shortly after we gathered our things, the Battalion Commander's driver pulled up in his Humvee. We quickly through our bags in the back and jumped inside, closing the doors almost simultaneously. Once the driver pulled away from the barracks, the questions started to come. I stalled for time, choosing not to answer them so I wouldn't ruin the surprise as the Humvee drew closer and closer to the helipad.

The vehicle came to a stop near the pad, and just before exiting, I let the cat out of the bag—watching their excitement while fighting back my own and maintaining my composure as if I had been there before.

We loaded our bags into the helicopter, strapped ourselves in, and placed the flight helmets on our heads as instructed. As the engine started and the rotors began to pick up speed, we were airborne in no time. I could hardly contain myself.

For an enlisted soldier, this was the equivalent of executive air travel—reserved for the rich and famous.

My crew and I took turns listening to one another through the earpieces of our flight helmets, expressing our excitement as the summer air rushed through the helicopter's interior. The pilot's voice came across our earpieces, overriding our conversation, and he asked me a question. "SGT Payne, do you have any special requests?"

I am not one to wag my own tail or spike the football in the end zone; however, with little to no thought, I replied, "My section sergeant is on range dunnage detail—can you fly over and bank on my side?" The pilot responded, "Say no more, Sarge," as he navigated the helicopter in the direction of the soldiers walking the tank trails at double-arm intervals, retrieving expended 7.62-mm brass scattered along the range.

From a very low altitude, I could see the soldiers on dunnage detail with the clarity of an HD television fresh out of the box. The pilot executed a slow banking maneuver to the right, positioning me directly above the detail. SSG Hawkins looked upward as the helicopter flew overhead, and our eyes locked as I waved at him with the most devious grin one could imagine. After the pilot steadied the aircraft, I leaned back in my seat with a heart full of joy and deep reflection, taking in the view of the contoured landscape far above the trees all the way back to the installation.

The landing was cinematic, and the aircraft seemed to float out of the sky as the landing skids gently returned to the surface of the earth. After landing, my crew and I thanked the pilots for an amazing experience, grabbed our duffle bags, and stood clear of the helicopter as it lifted off the ground to return to the range. We stood there watching the aircraft until it was no longer visible to the naked eye. With no words to share in that moment, my crew and I exchanged what I can only describe as a three-man hug of triumph and mutual respect. We then picked up our duffle bags and went in three different directions to begin our unauthorized five-day pass.

CHAPTER FIVE
Enemies Become Footstools

During my time away from Fort Riley, I returned to Texas to spend time with the new friends I had met during the Basic Non-Commissioned Officers Course a few months prior. Unfortunately, the days moved at the speed of light and the visit felt far too short. After four days and four nights of fun and relaxation in Killeen, Texas, it was time to return to work and face whatever challenges awaited me upon my return to Fort Riley.

Shortly after returning to work, I began to feel the weight of renewed scrutiny and found myself desiring a change of environment. A few weeks after our triumphant 1,000-point gunnery, I was sitting alone in the dining facility having breakfast when a fellow NCO joined me at the table. Because I had not seen him in some time, I asked where he was currently working. He explained that he had been reassigned to the Commanding General's Mounted Color Guard.

This was my second tour of duty at the fort, and until that moment, I had never heard of the Mounted Color Guard.

Intrigued, I began asking questions to gather as much information as I could about the potential opportunity. From what I learned, the Mounted Color Guard was having difficulty recruiting African American soldiers who could ride horses and was on an all-out mission to add diversity to what was then a predominantly white unit. I became convinced that this assignment would be the perfect change of environment I needed. There was only one problem—I had never ridden a horse in my entire life.

My fellow Sergeant was a country boy from Mississippi who had been raised on a farm. Riding a horse came as naturally to him as breathing, and he volunteered to teach me. Never one to shy away from a challenge, I accepted his offer. A few days later, I found myself inside a horse stable, looking completely out of place—not because I was a Black man, but because I stood out like a sore thumb in sneakers, dressed as if I were headed to the gym to play a few games of basketball.

My Army buddy's approach to teaching me how to ride was very methodical and slow—almost to the point where I grew bored and began to wonder if this would turn out to be a waste of my time.

He started at ground level, first teaching me about the tack and how to properly care for it. He also explained the gear I would need to purchase if I wanted to be taken seriously as a rider.

My second week of horseback lessons consisted of what he called *groundwork*. Groundwork involved walking a horse much like a dog owner would walk a pet to the park to socialize with other animals in the neighborhood. During this phase, I also learned how to properly care for a horse by washing and grooming it, cleaning the stalls, and using a hoof pick to remove manure from the frog of the horse's hooves. Eventually, the day came when I finally rode a horse. It was in a corralled area just outside the stable—where I would one day unknowingly re-enlist in the Army to extend my career. After a few outings in the corral, I began to feel comfortable with my ability to perform the basic riding techniques required to pass the riding evaluation for selection to Fort Riley's Commanding General's Mounted Color Guard. The very next day, I went out with a group of riders for my first experience riding in open country, and to say I was scared would be an understatement.

Reenlistment tradition

Photography: Valerie Bontrager

Sgt. John Payne, left, reenlists for the third time as Lt. Col. Melanie Reeder conducts the ceremony Wednesday afternoon. Payne is a member of the Commanding General's Mounted Color Guard and he is the fourth soldier to re-enlist while on horseback and dressed in traditional civil war era uniform at Fort Riley. The stable in the background, which currently houses the horses, was built in 1889.

Sgt Payne reenlisting on horseback

New to horseback riding, I had no idea how intelligent horses were. Toward the end of what had been a leisurely ride, the riders allowed their horses to really open up into a full gallop.

Up until this point, the ride had been going extremely well, and I felt confident in my ability to control a horse—until we reached a long, flat strip of land down in a valley beneath the road above. The horses began to grow excited as we lined up into two rows to race between a long line of electrical powerline poles.

Without any warning—or any signal from me—the horse I was riding took off, leaving me hanging on for dear life. The harder I pulled back on the reins, the faster he seemed to gallop, completely ignoring all of my commands, both physical and verbal. He went into autopilot and had his way with me.

The Color Guard members would race each other for the length of two telephone poles, turn around, and then race back in the opposite direction. The horse I was on had no regard for the fact that I was sitting on his back, and I could feel my anxiety building as it grew closer to the time for him to run again.

There were twelve of us on horseback that day—but only eleven riders. Everything I thought I knew about riding meant nothing in comparison to the seasoned riders around me.

All of the guys had previous riding experience, and most of them had been raised on farms, making them no strangers to the nuances of horseback riding. I remember that several were born and raised in Texas, while others rounded out the group from Mississippi and California—and then there was me, a novice at best, hoping to learn enough to be accepted as a member of the team.

My adrenaline began flooding my veins as the horse moved closer to the front of the line, almost trotting in place. If I had never truly respected horses before, I was quickly humbled on that day. The horse and I were now at the front, facing a long stretch of flat terrain covered in green grass, with ten horses and ten riders waiting behind us. I silently prayed this would be the last sprint of the day.

The horse's front hooves briefly left the ground as he reared just enough to gain forward momentum, shifting all of his weight onto his hind legs before darting off the line as if we were competing in the Baltimore Preakness.

I held on for dear life to where the saddle horn would have been—except McClellan Cavalry saddles don't have horns.

I could feel the power and majesty of the animal with every gallop as we charged toward the group waiting at the other end.

With absolutely no control over the situation, the horse eventually slowed from a gallop to a canter, then to a trot, and finally to a walk—giving me firsthand experience with each gait of his power.

Just as I gathered my seat on the pringle of a saddle, the group of riders headed back in the direction of the stable, and I couldn't have been more relieved.

Commanding Generals Mounted Color Guard, Main Street, Junction City, KS, July 1995.

I rode quietly in the back, watching this band of brothers enjoy their camaraderie away from the normal, everyday life of a soldier. In that moment, I knew I would need to learn much more about riding horses if I was going to pass the riding test and earn my place as a member of this group of horseback riders.

My fellow Sergeant continued working with me until I felt comfortable as a rider. Eventually, I took—and passed—the riding test and was selected to become a member of Fort Riley's Commanding General's Mounted Color Guard.

Becoming a member of the Mounted Color Guard was unlike anything I had ever imagined doing in life. We traveled throughout the Midwestern United States, riding in rodeos, parades, retirement ceremonies, and demonstrations. I enjoyed all of the activities, but the parades and demonstrations were my favorite.

The demonstrations allowed me to showcase the riding skills and talents I had worked so hard to develop. However, SSG Hawkins—and the trouble he stirred up—was never far away.

From time to time, I would run into guys from my old unit, and none of them could refrain from sharing updates about the fallout from SSG Hawkins's failed attempt to end my military career.

The Fallout

As Sir Isaac Newton's third law of motion states, to every action there is an equal and opposite reaction the pendulum effects of what SSG Hawkins put in place had started coming back and it would not be good for anyone standing close to him during the fallout. One day after getting off work or a day of fun because I didn't consider my time with the mounted color guard as work, I went to the Post Exchange to see if there were any new items on the shelves. I ran into my previous First Sergeant (1SG), and he could not wait to fill me in on what was going on back at my old unit.

On all major military installations, the government offers opportunities for military personnel and their family members to shop for groceries and other goods at a discounted rates and normally 10 to 15% cheaper than what is offered outside the gates on the economy.

During the gunnery exercise each Bradley Commander was issued a set amount of ammunition to complete the course, and it was strictly monitored and accounted for. After the exercise is concluded the Commanders were held responsible for turning in any ammunition left over.

SSG Hawkins was given extra ammunition to provide him with a competitive advantage over the rest of us participating in the gunnery exercise. To prevent discovery of his dishonesty, he gave the leftover 25-mm rounds to the driver of his Bradley and instructed him to get rid of them.

In a world driven by masculinity and bravado, the allure of that opportunity was too strong for a young, twenty-something Private to resist. Wanting to show off to a civilian friend, he decided to take advantage of the moment.

Fort Riley offered very few places for young people to gather and socialize, and Aggieville was one of them. Aggieville was a small strip of clubs, bars, and restaurants that catered to students from Kansas State University and soldiers from Fort Riley.

Once the sun dipped below the horizon, young people of every race, nationality, and educational background could be found congregating in that small microcosm. While out in Aggieville testing the limits of his newfound adulthood, SSG Hawkins's young and naïve driver was pulled over by a Manhattan, Kansas police officer for driving erratically.

The soldier was found to have alcohol in his system—which, as it turned out, was the least of his problems.

To add insult to injury, a quick search of his CJ-5 Jeep revealed a linked belt of 25-mm high-explosive rounds—an offense that would end his career before it had barely begun. The young soldier was arrested and did not hesitate to inform the authorities that his supervisor had given him the oversized rounds and instructed him to get rid of them. Wanting to show off a little before doing so, he chose the worst possible moment. It was never clear how he planned to dispose of the dangerous ammunition, but unfortunately for him, time had run out. I would like to believe this was the undefeated and undisputed record of karma claiming her victory for the wrongs that had been aimed at destroying me earlier that year.

I couldn't resist asking the First Sergeant (1SG) whether any well-deserved punishment was headed SSG Hawkins's way for the trap he had set for me. Apparently, he would be receiving a letter of reprimand placed in his permanent record—an action expected to have severe consequences for his career.

It was anticipated that it would likely prevent him from reaching his next level of promotion and eventually force him out of the military.

Strange thing about the first ten years of a twenty-year military career. No one wants to be forced out, and everyone suddenly wants to re-enlist when that option appears to be slipping away. My former First Sergeant informed me that my crew and I would be receiving the Army Commendation Medal for the 1,000-point gunnery. The most rewarding part, however, was learning that the award citation had been written by SGT Hawkins himself.

I was told that he had been forced to make corrections and revisions to the write-up several times until it met the standard the First Sergeant felt it should have met. Shortly after my encounter with my old 1SG, I was called back to my previous unit for the award ceremony.

I received the Army Commendation Medal in front of the entire battalion—with SSG Hawkins in attendance.

ATTENTION TO ORDERS! For meritorious achievement as the Bradley Commander of A-33. Sergeant Payne scored a perfect 1000 points on Bradley Table VIII during Level 1 Gunnery. His ability to engage and destroy targets as a crewmember of a Cavalry Fighting Vehicle greatly enhance the warfighting capabilities of his unit. His efforts reflect great credit upon himself, "The QUARTERHORSE," and the United States Army. Period of Service 25 February 1995 Through 16 March 1995.

Army Commendation Medal for Bradley Table VIII Gunnery Exercise

CHAPTER SIX
A CHANGE IN PERSPECTIVE

Never one to overstay my welcome, I began looking for my next career move. I knew that if I stayed with the Commanding General's Mounted Color Guard for too long, it would not be good for my career advancement. I have always believed that if you do not find something purposeful to do, someone else will determine your path for you. With that in mind, I started planning what I wanted to do next and how to make it happen within the constraints and limitations of a military environment.

Ever since Basic Training, I had admired Drill Instructors and set becoming one as a personal goal to accomplish before leaving the Army for civilian life. A few of my peers had already attended Drill Sergeant School and shared their lesson plans and stories from their time on Drill Sergeant duty—what they referred to as "the trail."

I made up my mind that becoming a Drill Sergeant would be my next move. I obtained the phone number for my branch office and called to inquire about the availability of a slot for a young Sergeant to attend the Drill Sergeant Instructor Course.

My branch officer stated that there were no slots available for Sergeants (E-5s) at the time, but there were vacancies for me to become a Recruiter. I quietly assessed my alternatives and concluded that I could do both. I would become a Recruiter, and when my tour of duty was up, I would double back and become a Drill Instructor—but that would never happen. I was never able to confirm the validity of the information my branch provided me, but I suppose it all worked out in the end. Before I knew it, I received orders to attend the Army Recruiting and Retention School in Columbia, South Carolina. After graduating from the United States Army Recruiting and Retention School, I was assigned to the Raleigh Recruiting Battalion with duty in Salisbury, North Carolina. I could hardly wait to get started.

While on vacation, I scheduled additional time to spend a day or two in nearby Charlotte, North Carolina, which is a short thirty-minute drive from Salisbury. I wanted to get a look at the location where I would be starting my recruiting career. After arriving in Charlotte the night before, I awoke early the next morning and rode around Salisbury to get a feel for the environment I would be working in for the next several years.

Taking Exit 76 off I-85 North, I entered the town of Salisbury and immediately realized I would be extremely miserable in this environment day in and day out. I was deeply disappointed with the location. The Army uses the acronym *I.A.W.*, which stands for *In Accordance With* and is usually followed by the phrase "the needs of the Army." This was one of those moments when its meaning became crystal clear to me. The Army did not care about my feelings regarding the assignment—only whether it had enough manpower to accomplish its mission.

As I rode around the town of Salisbury, I could feel my inner flame being doused. I imagined long, depressing days and nights of living there. My next stop was the recruiting station, where I hoped to meet the other recruiters and the Station Commander to see if anything might change my initial impression of the place.

The recruiting station was not hard to find at all. It was located off the main street, less than a mile from the interstate, and stood out like a sore thumb—as if it were screaming, *"Hello, we're over here!"*

In hindsight, I suppose that was exactly what the Army was going for, providing the best possible return on its marketing dollars.

It was one of those hot, thick, muggy days beneath clear Carolina-blue skies. It was so hot that my glasses fogged up as I exited the cool, air-conditioned interior of my car. Always wanting to project strength and walk in my authority, I opened the door of the recruiting station and closed it behind me. As I entered, I heard one of the Sergeants ask, "Can I help you?" I explained who I was and my purpose, and the Station Commander swiftly emerged from behind his desk to greet me with a handshake. He began providing information about the station and the role I would play once my leave was up. He spoke about market demographics, schools, cost of living, and several other factors any good recruiter would need to understand in order to be effective in accomplishing his or her monthly recruiting quota.

We talked for several minutes before shaking hands and parting ways. I beelined to my car before I could break out into a full sweat from the North Carolina humidity and immediately cranked up the air conditioner. Settled into my seat, seatbelt fastened, air blasting, and back on I-85 driving south toward Charlotte, my initial feelings about Salisbury remained unchanged by anything I had seen or heard during my short visit.

As I set my cruise control and settled into the drive, I knew I would have to do something drastic to alter the course of my near future and avoid what I was certain would be the absolute worst location for me to thrive personally or achieve any measure of recruiting success. Almost in a daydream, I stared at the highway, contemplating what my next move would be—when it came to me. Unsure whether it would work or not, I knew exactly what I had to do. I would have to drive to the Battalion Headquarters, talk to someone, and plead my case as to why I should be placed in a metropolitan area like Charlotte rather than a small, sparsely populated town like Salisbury.

After arriving back in the city, I stopped at a barbershop and patiently waited my turn to get a haircut. Still deep in thought, I silently rehearsed what I would say when I arrived at headquarters. Once my haircut was finished, I grabbed a bite to eat and returned to the hotel to prepare my uniform for the next day.

In true military fashion, I arose early. And as one of my favorite people—the 44th President of the United States, Barack Hussein Obama—would say, I was *fired up and ready to go*.

The next morning, my alarm went off and my feet hit the ground like a man with a mission. I jumped into the shower, took care of my personal hygiene, took my time, and donned my uniform with a great deal of pride before walking out into the world filled with optimism.

Before leaving town on what I calculated to be a two-hour and forty-five-minute drive, I stopped at a gas station to grab a cup of coffee and reviewed my map one last time before putting the car in drive. With my map on the passenger seat, the radio blasting, and a hot cup of gas-station coffee in hand, I was once again headed north on Interstate 85. This time, however, I was determined to try and alter what I believed to be a foregone conclusion—one that was well worth the attempt. The drive wasn't nearly as bad as I had imagined, and I arrived in almost record-breaking time. With coffee, music, and my thoughts to keep me company, I pulled up to my destination just as I was starting to feel the fatigue of the drive. After parking in the back of the lot, I gave myself a quick once-over to ensure my appearance was above reproach and met military standards before heading toward the front door of the six-story building.

After checking the directory in the lobby to locate the Battalion Headquarters, I stepped into the elevator and pressed the button for the third floor.

When the doors opened, I proceeded toward a set of glass double doors, reading every nameplate along the way as quickly as I could without appearing lost. Without breaking my stride, I noticed the titles and names of the Battalion Commander and Battalion Sergeant Major posted outside a single office. I walked in as if I had been there before.

Just inside the entrance sat the receptionist, and a few feet behind her were two office doors. The door on the left—the only one open—belonged to the Command Sergeant Major. Without hesitation, I approached the receptionist and, with a voice of assurance and confidence, said, "Good morning. My name is Sergeant John Payne, and I would like to speak with the Sergeant Major."

She asked if I had an appointment, but before I could respond, a voice rang out from the open office. "Who is that?" the Sergeant Major called.

I answered back just as confidently, "My name is SGT John Payne, Sergeant Major!"

Before I could finish my statement, the Sergeant Major was standing in the doorway of his office. Looking directly at me, he asked, "What can I help you with, Chief?"

"Chief" was a term older soldiers used as either a sign of respect or disrespect, depending entirely on the context in which it was delivered. If you were ever called Chief, you would instantly know the intent by the inflection in the speaker's voice. I wasn't completely sure how he meant it that day because I blew past his comment with my response, driven by my focus and determination to be heard.

The rank of Command Sergeant Major is the highest an enlisted member can achieve. However, when addressing them in conversation, you are well within protocol to refer to them simply as *Sergeant Major*. I knew I wouldn't get another chance to state my case, and if I truly wanted his attention, a little strategic flattery was in order. So, I reached for what I knew to be the ultimate compliment you can give a senior Non-Commissioned Officer—addressing them by their full military rank.

"Command Sergeant Major, I am assigned to your battalion, currently on leave and due to sign in in a few weeks, and I would like to speak with you about my current assignment."

He stood in the doorway with a look of confusion before inviting me into his office to have a seat. I explained that I was assigned to the Salisbury, North Carolina Recruiting Station and shared that I had visited the town and met the Station Commander the day prior. I then proceeded with the unwritten script I had rehearsed in my head over and over since my drive back to Charlotte after leaving Salisbury—and again during my drive that very morning.

"Command Sergeant Major, after visiting the Salisbury Recruiting Station, I believe placing me there would be an injustice to the Raleigh Recruiting Battalion and a waste of my talents as a recruiter. My skills would better serve your battalion if I were assigned to a metropolitan area such as Charlotte."

After I finished pleading my case—which felt more like pleading for my life—an awkward silence filled the room. We sat there staring at one another, each daring the other to look away.

I think he could see my determination, because he finally broke the silence by ordering me to the position of attention.

I stood up tall, as if I had just graduated from Basic Training earlier that day. He then instructed me to perform a series of facing movements until I was standing with my back to him, facing the wall.

After a few more facing movements, we were standing face-to-face once again, and he told me to relax and take my seat. I have always tried to extract lessons from every situation, and that day I learned the importance of consistency. With a stern look on his face, he asked, "Sergeant, do you always put edge dressing on your shoes?"

Without hesitation, I replied, "Is there any other way to wear them, Sergeant Major!" A small smirk crossed his face, and in that moment, I knew my persistence had paid off.

"Sergeant, come with me," he said.

I followed him down the hallway into the administrative personnel office, where he ordered the Sergeant in charge to amend my orders and assign me to the Charlotte Recruiting Station. He then turned to me and said, "SGT Payne, I expect you to make mission—or I am going to fire you!"

With a firm handshake, he turned and walked back to his office.

I finished up in the administrative office and took my time getting back to my car, moving as if it were business as usual—though inside I felt as if I might self-combust from happiness. No coffee was required on my return trip. The adrenaline from that moment of triumph carried me all the way back to Charlotte and lingered for hours afterward.

Still riding high from securing the assignment I had fought for, I made a stop by the Charlottetown Recruiting Station, which at the time was located in uptown Charlotte, North Carolina. Still in uniform, I walked into the office like I owned the place. As soon as I crossed the threshold, I noticed a senior NCO sitting at a desk near the back of the room. Without looking up, he quickly asked, "How can I help you, Chief?" By his tone, I knew immediately he was being facetious, but I paid it no mind. Instead, I answered with the confidence of someone who had nothing to lose and felt incapable of failing.

"My name is SGT Payne, and I will be assigned here soon. I just wanted to stop by and see the place before I started."

He laughed, and a few of the other Sergeants in the room joined in. Reaching into the top drawer of his desk, he pulled out a camera and said, "I want to take your picture!" I posed as he pressed the button on a Polaroid camera. He held the photo carefully by its edge, taking extra precaution not to touch the surface as the image developed.

Then he said, "You'll see this picture again, young whippersnapper. Now get on out of here—we've got work to do!"

I responded as I should. "Roger that, Sarge," I said, as I made my exit to the parking lot—satisfied with my efforts and the decision that had placed me exactly where I felt I belonged.

THE MEPS FAIRY

A true man of my word, I hit the ground running. After my first week on the job, I already had several people committed to enlisting in the Army. It quickly became apparent that I was a natural. For the first time in my life, I had found something I was both good at and genuinely enjoyed doing. Up until that moment, those two elements had never lived in the same house for me—let alone in the same neighborhood.

Preparing someone for enlistment is an intricate process with many moving parts, but engendering a commitment from the very start came second nature to me.

I would soon learn, however, that there was some behind-the-scenes magic required to prepare an applicant for processing at the Military Entrance Processing Station—affectionately known as the MEPS. The process began with prospecting: finding someone willing to talk to you about the Army and what it had to offer. Prospecting took many forms, including face-to-face interactions, telephone calls, and my personal favorite—area canvassing, to name a few. While prospecting, the primary objective was to schedule an appointment, taking care to provide just enough information to secure agreement, whether that appointment took place at the recruiting station or during a house call. Somewhere toward the end of the presentation, you had to ask for a commitment to join.

Then came the application phase—verification of documents such as a high school diploma, social security card, birth certificate, police checks, local drug testing, application completion, pre-testing, and finally, scheduling for the MEPS.

I must have been asleep during this part of the course because I remember absolutely nothing about it and swore it hadn't been covered during my time at the Recruiting and Retention School.

As proud as I wanted to be, I took my time preparing my first applicant to enlist in the Army, almost looking down my nose at the other recruiters. This would be one of those moments when my overconfident self would have to eat an extra-large slice of humble pie. I wish you could have seen me strutting past the other recruiters in the office as I turned in my packet for quality-control review.

I had all the necessary documentation neatly tucked into the pockets on both sides of the folder, just as I had been taught in school. Later that afternoon, I left the recruiting station to pick up my applicant and transport him to the hotel for an early start to the enlistment process the next morning.

After dropping him off, I walked back into the office practically dancing. I quickly prepared to head out for the day but couldn't resist taking a moment to talk a little trash to the other recruiters who were busy making phone calls in search of appointments.

I had a field day joking about their lack of recruiting talent and how much I hated making phone calls. The competitive nature of the office caused others to join in on the trash-talking until the senior recruiter finally ordered me out the door.

The next morning would come fast—and I couldn't wait to get back to the office.

The recruiting station was located in a nice office building on the corner of a major intersection in uptown Charlotte. Before walking into the office—or shortly thereafter—I would cross the street to an Exxon gas station and grab my morning cup of coffee.

This day was no different. When I pulled up, I walked over to the Exxon and made myself a large cup of coffee. To be honest, my cup was more sugar than coffee, but it always gave me a nice little jump-start to my day. With excitement in my demeanor, I sat at my desk as the other recruiters filed in one by one. I pretended to organize my paperwork, ticking like a time bomb, ready to pick up right where I had left off the day before. On most days, the Station Commander was the last person to come through the door.

She arrived like clockwork, greeting everyone as she walked past our desks toward her office at the back of the room. As soon as she set her bag down, the senior recruiter went into her office and closed the door. I could see them talking through the picture window, and I could just feel that the conversation was about me.

Shortly after the door opened and the senior recruiter returned to his desk, the Station Commander stood just outside her office and asked, "SGT Payne, did you schedule your applicant for the MEPS yesterday?"

As a new recruiter, I was completely unaware that scheduling an applicant for MEPS was even a thing. I answered her question with a question of my own.

"We have to schedule an applicant to go to the MEPS?" I asked.

"Yes!" she replied.

The conversation went around in circles for a while, with the senior recruiter adding a word or two here and there to keep the prank going.

At first, I thought they were playing a nasty trick on me, but as it dragged on, I began to believe I had made a serious mistake—and that because of my oversight, my applicant wouldn't be able to enlist that day. They let the joke go on just long enough to humble me a little, but it wouldn't last long.

The senior recruiter finally came clean just as I was on my way out the door to pick up my applicant from MEPS. I quickly put two and two together and realized he had scheduled my applicant for processing the evening prior—looking out for the office as a whole while saving my hide at the same time. Rhetorically, I asked, "Did you schedule my applicant for processing?"

With perfect comedic timing, he replied, "Who else did it—the MEPS Fairy?"

The entire office erupted in laughter at my expense, but I didn't care. I had just put my first applicant in the Army, and it was only my first week on the job. None of the other guys in the office could say the same, and I knew I had found something I was good at—and nothing was going to stop me from becoming successful at it.

MORNING CUP OF JOE

Other members of the station began to respect my talents as a recruiter and admired my ability to use different closing techniques to engender commitments from prospects to enlist in the Army.

A few of the guys would ask to ride out with me in hopes of capturing some of the recruiting magic they believed I had. What they didn't know was that I invested in civilian resources to broaden my knowledge of sales and closing techniques—materials I studied on my own time. When a recruiter faces the pressure of missing monthly quotas for several consecutive months, pride tends to go out the window, and it becomes easier to notice the recruiters who consistently hit their numbers. Before long, I started getting attention from some of the guys, and one of them suggested that we work together to make life a little easier.

I was presented with an offer that was difficult to overlook. The Sergeant proposed that if he could find two interested prospects, he would schedule the appointments, and I would close them. For every two I closed, he would allow me to put one of them in the Army as my applicants.

To provide proper context, the Sergeant was White, working in a predominantly Black population. His baritone voice made it easy for him to schedule appointments over the phone, but when he showed up at a prospect's home, he sometimes struggled to relate well enough to close the deal as often as he would have liked. I know it may sound like he was using me; however, the arrangement benefited me as well.

Besides, he and I were on the same team—and the Army doesn't see race, or at least that's what it would like you to believe. I was once told there were only two colors in the Army: light green and dark green. I believe it's unrealistic to group people of every background, nationality, and skin color into one organization and pretend that racial dynamics don't exist.

That said, Sergeant Murphy was a good egg. He would later become the best man in my wedding some years down the road. Murphy and I began walking across the street together each morning to get our first dose of caffeine. I would order a large cup of hazelnut coffee with a gallon of creamer and a pound of sugar, while Murphy stuck to his Mountain Dew.

One of my superpowers was my ability to establish rapport and develop working relationships with people who were instrumental in my success as a recruiter. I knew every recruiter from every branch of service who worked in the same building that I did. I developed those connections because I believed I was making a difference in the lives of the people I spoke with. If I couldn't help someone start a better way of life by joining the Army, I would not hesitate to introduce them to a recruiter from another branch if that meant they could still change their life for the better.

Many of the recruiters in the building warned me about the gas-station supervisor, suggesting he might be a racist. That didn't deter me from walking over each morning to get my first cup of coffee, but I did stay alert—keeping my eyes open and maintaining awareness to avoid any potential confrontation.

One morning, Murphy and I purchased our drinks and began what we jokingly called our conversational strategy meeting as we walked away from the store.

As we passed the gas pumps and headed toward the sidewalk to cross the street, I heard a voice call out my name. "SGT Payne, can I have a word with you?"

I turned to Murphy, reminding him of the whole dark-green/light-green thing, and asked him to watch my back. Both of us were confused, and I couldn't think of any reason this guy would want to talk to me about anything. Slowly, I turned around and retraced my steps back toward the gas station. The man and I met halfway between the sidewalk along the street and the gas pumps closest to the building.

With much apprehension, I asked the middle-aged, alleged racist, "What can I do for you, sir?" What he said next was completely unexpected and caught me totally off guard.

The gentleman explained that he had recently spoken with every recruiter from every branch of service in our building, and they had all told him the same thing. He said that if there was anyone who could help him, I was the guy. With a slight tremble in his voice, he added, "SGT Payne, I have lost my son to the streets, and I would like your help to get him back."

I asked him a few questions about his son to get an idea of what I would be up against and to determine whether it was even possible for me to help him get on a more positive path in life. After he answered my questions, I knew I could help the young man—but he would have to want my help. Convincing a young person that they need or could benefit from help is often the most difficult part of the job.

I told the concerned father that if he was serious about me trying to help his son, he would have him outside my office the next morning around 9:00 a.m., and I would see what I could do. He assured me that his son would be there. We shook hands, and I caught up with Murphy to walk back across the street and start our day of engendering commitments for enlistment into the U.S. Army.

The following morning, I woke early, prepared myself for work, and headed to my car, which was parked at the edge of the stairs just beyond the walkway outside my apartment door. The sun was bright, and the weather was warm enough for me to drive with the windows rolled down. Young, free, unapologetic, and overflowing with confidence, I drove with my music turned up loud.

Refusing to lower the volume of my stereo, I pulled into the parking lot of our office building, which housed the recruiting stations of all four major branches of the Armed Forces.

As I parked, I was reminded of the promise I had made to a father just the day before. Standing at the front of the building were the man and his son—right where he said they would be. I could see the anticipation on their faces as I walked across the parking lot to greet them and meet his son for the first time.

After just one glance at the young man, I immediately understood what the father meant when he said he had lost his son to the streets. The impressionable teenager appeared to be a walking contradiction. He was dressed like many of the Black urban kids in the area, and when he spoke, it gave me pause. If you relied on your ears alone, you would never believe he was a Caucasian kid from a rural North Carolina suburb.

Judging by his body language, I could tell he was not thrilled to be there. His loud outburst—"I'm not joining no damn Army!"—only confirmed what his posture and demeanor had already made clear.

Nevertheless, they both followed me inside. I pulled an extra chair up to my desk, and as we all sat down, I formally introduced myself. They did the same.

The young man's father checked his ego at the door, and I could tell he would do almost anything—short of going to jail—for his son to have a decent shot at a productive adulthood. He broke the ice by introducing them both. "SGT Payne, I'm Robert Massey, and this is my son, Thomas Massey."

As if I hadn't heard him the first time, Thomas reiterated his feelings about his father's staged intervention. This time, he raised his voice with more confidence and volume than before—loud enough for anyone on the first floor to hear. "I'm not joining no damn Army!"

This time was different. Just as he finished the last syllable of the last word, I responded with twice the aggression he had displayed. "YOU DON'T QUALIFY TO JOIN THE ARMY!"

You would not have believed the expressions of shock on their faces. From that moment on, I had Thomas's undivided attention. Mr. Massey looked as if his son's last opportunity to make something of himself had slipped away, while Thomas sat in stunned silence.

I informed them both that we would not be talking about the Army that day because doing so would be a waste of my time.

I asked Thomas a few open-ended, fact-finding questions to confirm details I had already learned about him from another recruiter in a different branch across the hall. Like a physician, I offered my diagnosis and asked Thomas if he wanted to finish school. He replied that he did.

I stood up and asked them both to follow me outside. Standing in front of the building, I assured Mr. Massey that his son would be okay and that I would make sure he got home safely—but first, I needed to take him somewhere. Mr. Massey trusted me. He hugged his son, shook my hand, and went to work.

Less than a mile up the road was a community college, where I had excellent rapport with several educational counselors. Within a few hours, I had Thomas enrolled in an adult high school completion program. I wanted him to earn his high school diploma rather than settle for a GED.

Before we parted ways, I made myself available to Thomas if he needed a ride to school. I also let him know that I would be keeping track of his grades throughout the school year.

Still early when I returned to the office, Murphy and I walked across the street to keep our morning ritual intact. This time, however, Mr. Massey paid for both of our drinks as I briefed him on my plans for his son. Thomas attended school faithfully, and I would drop in to check on him at least two days a week, making sure he understood that I would be holding him accountable.

Eventually, Thomas landed a job at a McDonald's just a few yards up the road, on the same side of the street as the gas station where his father worked. Several times a week, I could count on Thomas walking through the office doors with bags of food. We could practically set our watches by his consistency, and all the recruiters dreaded the day he would finally join the Army and ship off to Basic Training—for fear of losing our free hamburgers and hot fries.

Thomas worked hard in school, earning good grades and maintaining excellent attendance. The school year went by in a flash, and before I knew it, graduation was just around the corner.

After putting in a school years' worth of effort, Thomas stopped by the recruiting station to give me an invitation to his commencement ceremony. I assured him that I would be there and told him how much I was looking forward to witnessing his big day.

I had grown accustomed to Thomas being around and could feel that our time together was coming to an end. Being a man of my word, I attended his commencement ceremony and watched this young man accomplish something I imagine his father once doubted he ever would.

After the ceremony, I waited patiently to greet Thomas and present him with the gift I had purchased shortly after he gave me the invitation.

When selecting his gift, I flashed back to my own time in Basic Training and the one item I had treasured and relied on the most. I knew it would come in handy for Thomas as well—even though he hadn't enlisted in the Army yet. Drawing from my own military experience, I chose a watch that glowed in the dark, displayed military time, and had an alarm.

Not only was Thomas happy to see me there, but he was also genuinely surprised that I had given him a gift to commemorate such an important achievement in his life. I reached out to shake his hand, and that gesture turned into a hug. I hugged Thomas like a proud big brother.

Of all the thoughts racing through his mind in that moment, amid all the excitement, Thomas leaned in and spoke directly into my ear.

"Can we talk about the Army now?"

I knew right then that he had carried that question as fuel through an entire school year. He had earned my full attention and was no longer a waste of my time. More importantly, he was now qualified to enlist—not only in the Army, but in any branch of the Armed Forces. I congratulated Thomas and encouraged him to enjoy his graduation. We agreed to talk the following week, after he finished his weekend of celebration.

The weekend passed, and as a creature of habit, I pulled into the parking lot and exited my car the same way I had so many times before.

Thomas had returned from his weekend of celebration and was standing at the entrance of the building, just as he and his father had done nearly a year earlier when we first met. Only this time, he wasn't yelling, "I'm not joining the damn Army!" Instead, he was excited to see me and eager to move forward with the rest of his life.

Thomas opened the door for me and followed me inside, asking, "Can we talk about the Army now?" I said yes and gave him one of my best presentations—leaving nothing out and taking no shortcuts. I wanted Thomas to be fully informed so he could make the best possible decision for himself.

Immediately after my presentation, Thomas agreed to enlist. We completed his application that very day, and before the week was over, he had enlisted in the Army. After enlisting, Thomas spent a few weeks in the Delayed Entry Program before departing for Basic Training. Two weeks came and went, and it was getting closer to the time when he would be leaving home for the first time to begin his Army career. A few days before Thomas was scheduled to depart, I was standing in the gas station paying for my morning cup of coffee, talking with Mr. Massey as he shared how proud he was of his son.

Before I could leave, he invited me to a party he was hosting to see Thomas off to Basic Training. He would not take no for an answer, and I gave him my word that I would be there as I made my exit to start the day.

Because of the heavy demands placed on me as a recruiter, I learned how to blend my personal life with my professional life. My girlfriend and I already had plans, so I asked if she would accompany me to the Masseys' home before we carried out our plans for the evening. She humored me. We dressed for our night together and agreed to stop by, mingle briefly, and then leave to enjoy the rest of our evening.

I can count on one hand the number of times I have truly been afraid, and this was one of them. As I drove closer to the Masseys' home, my surroundings stirred memories of Mr. Massey's past feelings toward people who look like me. Not only was I fearful for myself, but I had now added my girlfriend to a situation that had the potential to become a racial disaster.

Everything around me fed those thoughts—the part of town we were in, the homes, the neighborhood, and the people who lived there. Each detail served as a reminder of the risk I was taking.

I pulled up to the Masseys' home cautiously and parked strategically, just in case I needed to leave in haste because of some unfortunate act, comment, or uncomfortable moment rooted in racism. Once I was satisfied with my parking strategy, I shut off the engine and escorted my girlfriend to the front door. We could hear what sounded like a good time happening on the other side.

Gathering my nerves, I knocked on the door as if I were entering a conference room for a promotion board—or like a police officer arriving to make an arrest.

Mr. Massey opened the door and warmly greeted my girlfriend and me, inviting us inside. The initial part of the visit was a blur, but I distinctly remember feeling extremely uncomfortable. It felt as though my girlfriend and I were the only people of color within a fifty-mile radius. We did our best to blend in with the rest of the guests and avoid drawing any unwanted attention to ourselves.

It appeared that everyone—except my girlfriend and me—was intoxicated and having the time of their lives.

With his speech slurred, Mr. Massey tried to get everyone's attention but was ignored at first. Still, he persisted. Standing in the middle of his living room, he finally yelled, "EVERYBODY, SHUT THE HELL UP!"

This time, he had everyone's attention. The room grew so quiet I could hear my heart pounding in my ears. Mr. Massey walked closer to me, and I could smell the alcohol on his breath. He placed his hand on my shoulder, which made me extremely uncomfortable.

What he said next, however, was unexpected—and it eased my tension just enough for me to lower my guard. Mr. Massey explained to his guests that he had a statement to make. "This man has done something for me that no one else was able to do," he said. "He gave my son back to me!"

Then he looked directly at me, as if we were the only two people in the room. With tears in his eyes, he added, "You have changed my feelings toward Black people."

I once heard that babies and drunks tell the truth. He was far from his infant years, so I took it as a win. A quick glance out the window showed the sun dipping toward the horizon, and I knew I didn't want to be caught driving through this small Carolina town after dark. I thanked Mr. Massey for the invitation and offered a condensed version of our plans for the evening.

Clutching my girlfriend's hand, we made our way to the front door and beelined back to my strategically parked car. I drove out of town cautiously, doing my best to avoid any unwanted attention from the authorities.

The day finally came for Thomas to ship out to Basic Training. Before he left my sight, he asked me to promise that I would attend his graduation ceremony after completing training. I assured him that I would.

CHAPTER SEVEN
A CHANGE OF DUTY STATION

Seventy-Nine Romeo

There are several recruiter traits and characteristics that become noticeable among recruiters, and when you are truly good at the job, those traits tend to reveal themselves to the civilian population as well. The majority of Army recruiters are assigned to recruiting duty temporarily, and many would rather deploy to a war zone than endure a tour as an Army Recruiter because of the immense pressure to meet daily, monthly, and quarterly enlistment requirements.

During my thirteen-year tenure as an Army Recruiter, I categorized recruiters into four distinct types based on their effort and outcomes. The first—and least desirable—category is "The Unwilling." The Unwilling were soldiers who would have preferred to do almost anything other than recruit, and they made up a significant portion of the recruiting workforce at the time. Many of them would go so far as to sabotage their own military careers in hopes of being released early from recruiting duty.

My second category is "The Survivor." The Survivor flew just below the radar, doing only enough to get by while counting the days until their recruiting tour finally came to an end.

My third category is "The Natural." This is the category I believe best described my entry into the field of recruiting. From the beginning, I had a genuine desire to be successful, and the art of recruiting came naturally to me.

The final category is "The Closer." The Closer represents the elite—the cream of the crop. This group mastered the art of overcoming objections, identifying unexpected needs, and turning prospects into applicants by convincing them that the Army offered something they either needed or wanted. Closers could sell almost anything. Sergeant First Class Eddie Edwards was one of those personalities and, during my tenure, one of the best Closers in the business.

As an Army Recruiter, I had never felt as fulfilled doing anything else up to that point in my life. Although the job was tough and challenging, it came to me naturally.

Even more so, I developed my own nuances that consistently produced the results I was looking for. During my first year on recruiting duty, my supervisor monitored my activities closely to ensure I was operating within the guidelines of the Battalion's New Recruiter Program. As part of that program, the battalion would occasionally send out a Master Trainer to assess a recruiter's ability to make and conduct appointments, as well as process applicants for enlistment. Eventually, it was time for me to receive my evaluation, and they sent one of their most experienced and well-respected trainers—Sergeant First Class Eddie Edwards.

I received notification of Eddie's arrival early Monday morning to begin what would be my final evaluation as a new recruiter. The weekend disappeared quickly, as most did for a young man who lived for his time off and away from work.

I arrived in the recruiting station's parking lot in the same ritualistic fashion I had followed so many mornings before—music loud, windows rolled down. I always enjoyed my morning drives to work almost as much as the evening drives home after a long day.

Happy for no reason other than the sun was shining and the sky was blue, I walked into the office to find my Station Commander having a pleasant conversation with the Master Trainer. Both were clearly waiting for my arrival to begin the evaluation.

In my customary way, I greeted everyone within the sound of my voice and took a seat at my desk to gather myself for the day's events. Sergeant Edwards approached and asked, "Are you ready to get started, Payne?"

"Absolutely!" I replied.

I enjoyed the freedom and autonomy of prospecting in the community more than any other recruiting method—especially when the weather was good. This would be one of those summer days that reminded me of home in Florida, with the sun hitting my face just right.

Sergeant Edwards laid out the rules of engagement for my evaluation, and to my surprise, he allowed me to be myself. He wanted a true and accurate representation of how I conducted my day-to-day business. Although I didn't know him personally before that day, I felt comfortable enough to operate as I normally would.

I gathered what I called my *kit bag*—a small duffel filled with brochures, twenty-five-count bundles of business cards, and several stacks of door hangers to leave behind for those cold-knock attempts that ended with no answer. After reviewing my list of follow-ups, I selected a few prospects for cold door knocks, buckled my seatbelt, and headed out into the community.

Attempt after attempt produced the same result, and the mercury climbed higher as the day wore on. Sergeant Edwards and I agreed that I would make one more attempt before breaking for lunch. After a quick review of my map and the next address on my list, I gathered my composure and headed to the final location.

As I entered the neighborhood, I spotted the house from a distance—a corner lot with a partial chain-link fence and a concrete slab along the side that doubled as a driveway, minus an attached two-car garage. As I pulled onto the driveway, Sergeant Edwards informed me that he would remain in the car with the air conditioning running while I knocked on the door. I was to let him know if there were any signs of life, and he would join me inside if I was lucky enough to be invited in.

Nearly certain this attempt would also be a waste of time; I placed the vehicle in park and grabbed a door hanger with my contact information—just in case someone at the residence had an interest in the Army or any of its programs. Expecting to be back quickly, I stepped out of the government-furnished vehicle, closing the door behind me and trading cool air for heat and humidity.

I walked around the right side of the house, climbed the steps to a small concrete platform, and knocked on the door—three firm knocks—then paused for a few seconds to see if anyone would respond. When there was no sign of movement inside, I knocked a second time. Still, no one came to the door or even glanced out a window.

Confident no one was home, I hung the door hanger and started my short walk back around the side of the house, my mind already on lunch. As I rounded the corner toward the car, I was startled by a dog standing directly in my path.

This was no ordinary dog. It was a German-bred Rottweiler, easily close to a hundred pounds. The beast and I locked eyes and froze in place. For a few seconds, nothing moved.

The world stood still as we silently sized each other up, both trying to figure out what would happen next.

The dog growled and lowered its head just as my fight-or-flight instincts kicked in—and I chose flight. It was obvious the dog had chosen violence and was fully prepared to defend its territory.

I came out the gate like an Olympic track star sprinting for gold, with the dog a close second, snapping at my heels. I was rapidly approaching the driver's side of the car while Sergeant Edwards watched the entire scene unfold from the comfort of the air-conditioned vehicle. At top speed, I rehearsed my plan: open the car door, dive inside, slam it shut, and live to recruit another day.

Just as I reached for the door handle to execute my well-rehearsed escape, Sergeant Edwards reached across the armrest from the passenger side and locked the door.

Without hesitation, I launched myself like Michael Jordan in Game Six of the 1992 NBA Finals, landing on the roof of the car—still in full uniform, complete with all my awards and decorations, long-sleeve AG-415 shirt, and a black necktie tied in a four-in-hand knot.

As the dog circled the car like something out of Tom and Jerry, I lay flat on my stomach, peering through the windshield, while Sergeant Edwards was sprawled across both front seats laughing uncontrollably, tears streaming down his face. I yelled at him through the glass for locking me out as he struggled to breathe between fits of laughter.

Eventually, the dog lost interest and wandered back toward the house. I quickly climbed down and slipped into the car before it could return for a second round of our real-life cartoon.

Once the dust—and laughter—settled, I asked Sergeant Edwards why he locked the door. Still on the verge of convulsing from laughter, he replied, "It didn't make sense for both of us to get ate up."

We laughed nonstop and could barely finish our lunch. At the end of the day, we made it back to the recruiting station, still laughing as we walked through the door. Needless to say, I received high marks on my evaluation and would later be asked to convert from my original military occupational specialty to become a permanent recruiter. I've known Mr. Eddie Edwards since the mid-1990s, and to this day, we still laugh every time we see each other.

Station Commander

My time as a Field Recruiter had come to an end, and it was time for me to move on. The United States Army Recruiting Command (USAREC) selected me for assignment as a Station Commander at the Havelock Recruiting Station. Havelock is located about a mile outside the front gate of Marine Corps Air Station Cherry Point, just minutes from the Atlantic Ocean and the Outer Banks of North Carolina. My success as a Field Recruiter had earned me the opportunity to supervise my own recruiting station, and I was determined to make the most of it. My new wife and I packed our belongings and headed to Coastal Carolina to begin a new chapter in Havelock, North Carolina.

While in Havelock, we lived in government housing on Marine Corps Air Station Cherry Point, centered directly off the main artery that runs through town. I acclimated to my new environment rather quickly and immediately focused on making my mark as a Station Commander by imprinting my recruiting philosophies and leadership style onto my soldiers. We came out of the gate fast.

My team was small—only four soldiers, including myself—but during my tenure, we accounted for more than 85 percent of the available market share for enlistments into the U.S. Army. Although we achieved measurable success, it did not come without sacrifice. At times, it required laying aside personal differences and enduring racial conflict, both inside and outside the office.

On many occasions, I had to prove my ability to engender commitments in order to gain the respect of the soldiers under my leadership—especially as a Black man recruiting in a predominantly Caucasian area. I have heard many people claim they are "colorblind," but I believe there is something deeply flawed in that ideology. To me, it aligns closely with cognitive dissonance.

In my opinion, we cannot move closer to racial equality until we open our eyes to see, recognize, respect, and acknowledge our differences. However, that is a story for another day. Working in this environment opened my eyes to the existence of hidden racism. It was an awakening for me, particularly given my devotion to—and indoctrination into—the Army's systems, rules, regulations, and lifestyle.

Not all rules are written in manuals, and many of the unwritten ones proved to be far more revealing and educational in the long term. One such unwritten philosophy that stayed with me was the military racial theory of *Dark Green* and *Light Green* soldiers. If you take the time to analyze that concept, as I have, you may come to the same conclusion: it is simply another ideology rooted in racial division.

Right Place, Wrong Time

The day finally came when I would come face-to-face with racism in a fashion I had never encountered before. That day reshaped my perception of my status as a human being in America, in the Army, and as a recruiter for the Army.

As a Station Commander, I viewed the end of each recruiting month like the final seconds of a championship basketball game—with the ball in my hands and the clock winding down. Although the month had been going well, a sense of panic began to set in as time slipped away. With one enlistment secured and only a few days left in the month, one of my soldiers all but dared me to ride along with him to showcase my closing ability so he could achieve his quota and, in turn, help the station meet its mission.

Without hesitation, I climbed into the passenger seat of my soldier's government-assigned vehicle, buckled my seatbelt, and prepared for the long drive into a marshy coastal area of Carteret County to influence a young man to join the Army. As we drove deeper into the swamp, the major roadway gave way to a much narrower stretch of asphalt—barely wide enough for two vehicles to pass in opposite directions. Small canals, filled halfway with water, lined both sides of the road.

As we arrived in the small town where the prospect lived with his parents, I noticed a large billboard that I might have overlooked under normal circumstances had it not been positioned so low to the ground. The sight of it immediately struck fear in me, but it was far too late to do anything other than conceal my reaction and pretend I hadn't seen what I had saw. The billboard was massive—something that should have stood twenty feet in the air—yet it sat only four or five feet above the ground.

I couldn't believe what I was looking at. It was an advertisement for the Ku Klux Klan.

Soon after passing the billboard, my soldier and I arrived at our destination—a modular home with low ceilings, thin walls, and an open floor plan.

Because of my uneasiness, I made quick work of the pleasantries as we sat down at the dining-room table and began my presentation. Just as my discomfort started to subside, a truck pulled into the driveway, and the prospect began showing signs of anxiety. I dismissed his uneasiness, assuming it was simply a distraction from the purpose that had brought us there.

The front door opened, and a middle-aged, heavyset white man entered the house carrying what appeared to be a lunchbox. He closed the door behind him, scanned the open floor plan. After briefly noticing my soldier and I seated at his dining-room table, he walked past us without acknowledgment, and sat down in a recliner angled toward the television.

His son, clearly nervous by his father's arrival, broke eye contact with us to acknowledge him as the man of the house. My soldier and I followed suit, offering a polite greeting—but our words were met with silence, as if we had said nothing at all.

Already feeling trapped between a rock and a hard place, I resolved to complete the mission and pressed forward with my presentation.

The gentleman's spouse beelined from the kitchen and welcomed her husband home for the evening of what seemed to be a hard day's work. She would bend over the chair to give him a kiss as she picked up his lunchbox from the table just beyond the armrest of the recliner he looked up at his wife and blurted out loud enough to ensure I could hear him, "what is that nigger doing in my house!" Any determination I had quickly dissolved, and I knew it was time for me to go.

My soldier turned to me and asked what I was going to do, and I knew my decision would have to be made quickly. I replied, loud enough to be heard throughout the length of the modular home, "this Nigger will be outside in the car!"

I asked my soldier for the keys to his government vehicle, told him to finish the presentation, and made a hasty retreat to the car. Unlocking the car, I jumped into the driver's seat, started the vehicle, and simultaneously adjusted the car seat while putting the car in drive.

I maneuvered the vehicle around the unpaved front yard until the car was facing the road.

I then adjusted all the mirrors so I could observe the front door and other angles, mitigating the risk of someone sneaking up on me from the rear of the car. Leaving the engine running, I sat there more nervous than I had ever felt—even compared to war in the Middle East.

With the radio off and nothing to keep me company but the sound of the engine wasting gas, I scanned my surroundings as the sun fell toward the horizon and darkness waited just beyond the edge of the woods, ready to cover us like a blanket on a cold night. With my head on a swivel and the headlights growing brighter, I noticed movement in the rearview mirror as the front door opened.

My soldier made an exit and beelined to the car. As he got closer, I placed the car in drive and started moving long before he could settle in or put on his seatbelt. The sun was sinking fast, and by this time the headlights were bright as ever. Although I was driving with purpose, I was extremely careful to obey the speed limit.

I did not want to get stopped in this area in broad daylight—let alone at night. I then took a moment to gather my composure before asking my soldier if he had closed the sale and engendered a commitment from the young man to enlist in the Army.

He enthusiastically told me that he had closed the sale and that the young man had agreed to enlist. Most importantly, he would accomplish his individual quota, and the station would achieve its mission. The ride back to the station was mostly quiet, as I used the travel time to unwind and decompress so I wouldn't take that energy home to my family.

I did not want my wife to live in fear by hearing about the events of my day, so I chose to protect her by keeping this information to myself. After all, it was because of my career that we were there in the first place, and it was my responsibility to keep my family safe. My soldier and I never talked about that event again, but I could not overlook the fact that he wasn't bothered by it at all. Instead, he took comfort in the acceptance he felt in an environment that I was not welcomed.

CHAPTER EIGHT
THE FOLLOW UP

What Ever Happen to Thomas?

Most of my tenure as a soldier in the Army was spent on recruiting duty, and while on recruiting duty, I met and married my wife. Because of that, she would meet some of my recruits but would hear stories about the rest of them. However, there were always a few who stood out for one reason or another, and the times our paths crossed stayed with us.

Every now and then, someone would come to mind, and I would wonder how they were getting along in their new careers as soldiers in the Army. Thomas was one of those memorable individuals whose interactions spilled over into my personal life—so much so that my wife would sometimes ask me, "Whatever happened to Thomas?" That question would spark conversations of yesteryear and provide a platform to talk about past experiences and old acquaintances we hadn't seen or heard from in years. No matter the topic of conversation, Thomas Massey's name would always come up.

The life of an Army Recruiter could feel like a revolving door of incomplete relationships.

Meeting different people daily in a cat-and-mouse game of serving and service, I quickly learned that all people are connected in some way. Meeting people is like navigating a never-ending, interconnected web of community that provides a simple—but necessary—means for serving one another. Everyone is a tool to be used for the greater good of the next person, each serving the other if it is done correctly. Sometimes, however, there are people who seek only to receive and do not reciprocate in kind. When that happens, alternate routes within the web must be discovered to facilitate the ultimate goal of serving the community and being served by the community. Mr. Massey is a great example of how communities can be connected. Our time shared for the greater good of his son's future caused him to connect with me, which ultimately expanded both of our communities. Although he may have held feelings toward those who look like me, his love for his son superseded any racial prejudice in his effort to save his son from the uncertainty of his current path in life.

Queen City Pit Stop

Each year during my time on active duty, I would schedule my annual leave during the month of August, when my wife was on summer break from the rigors of educating students and to celebrate my birthday on the ninth day of the month. Usually, my family and I would execute our vacation plan, which we affectionately called the "World Tour." The World Tour meant that wherever we resided, our vacation would include a trip to visit relatives in South Carolina before soaking up an abundance of vitamin D from the Florida sun and then returning home.

I always enjoyed our road trips because they gave me an opportunity to gaze at the beauty of the landscape as I drove up and down the eastern part of the United States. As we traveled, we would sometimes make stops in cities and towns we had lived in or frequented in the past. My wife and I both shared a love for the city of Charlotte, North Carolina, and although we had considered living there a few times, we would always make a pit stop whenever our travels took us along I-77 or I-85.

Even if only for a few minutes, we would stop to visit friends and family and stretch our legs before continuing on our way.

As we drew closer to the city on this particular trip, we found ourselves reminiscing about past events. The drive brought back memories of dating, getting married, my wife attending college, and several of the soldiers I had recruited, along with thoughts about where they might be in life.

Without fail, whenever the words *Charlotte* and *recruiting* came up together, one name always followed Thomas. I had spent a great deal of time with Thomas, and because of that, my wife and I felt as though we had known him for a long time.

As we entered York County, South Carolina, I decided to stop in Charlotte to fuel up and possibly grab a bite to eat before continuing north toward our destination in Upstate New York. During our conversation about Thomas, my wife turned to me and asked, "Do you think his father still works at that gas station on the corner across from your old job?" I replied, "I don't know." Without hesitation, she said, "You should stop by there."

I remember feeling a great deal of apprehension about visiting the gas station. This was during the Iraq War, and the news networks seemed to be broadcasting a steady stream of reports about servicemembers being killed every day. One of my greatest fears was running into a parent or loved one of someone I had recruited into the Army, only to learn that they had been killed in the line of duty. My wife, however, was persistent and became almost relentless as my SUV continued to close the distance to the gas station on the corner.

I finally gave in to her pressure. Once we reached the city limits, I took the exit and drove toward the old gas station, hoping the man had moved on or simply wasn't there that day. From a distance, I could see the gas station on the right side of the road as I crept down the street, pretending to admire the well-manicured, lush southern landscape. No matter how carefully I obeyed the city speed limit, the gas station seemed to be approaching fast. I activated my turn signal and eased into the nearly empty parking lot. Because my gas tank was on the driver's side, I was forced to pull up to the inner set of pumps, which placed me closer to the front door of the convenience store where Thomas's father usually stood.

Almost hiding, I exited the driver's seat and moved to the rear of my SUV to remove the gas cap, peering through the slightly tinted windows as my family walked into the store.

And before I could pull my wallet from my back pocket, I heard someone yell out, "Payne!" Thomas's dad had recognized me and came running out of the building, speed-walking between the gas pumps until he was standing in front of me. My fight-or-flight sensors were broken, and I just stood there as if my shoes were glued to the pavement, wondering what was going to happen next.

After confirming it was me, his face softened. He extended his hand, and as soon as he got a firm grip, he pulled me toward him and gave me one of the biggest hugs I had received in recent memory. It was the kind of hug I had always imagined a father would give his son for some deed of approval. I was relieved that he was thrilled to see me; however, I was even more relieved to realize his son had not become a casualty of war.

Mr. Massey wasted no time with small talk and got straight to the topic of the moment. As he began talking about his son, he reached into his back pocket with his right hand and pulled out his wallet.

Once it was freed from his pocket, he positioned it in front of his body and, with his left hand, held up his billfold between his thumb and index finger, allowing the pictures inside to roll out like an accordion, nearly touching the ground between our feet.

With an expression of joy on his face, Mr. Massey went on and on about his pride in his son. Since the last time I had seen him, Thomas had married and made Mr. Massey one of the proudest grandfathers I had ever seen.

He started at the top and moved down to the bottom of his line of pictures as if he were pulling in a fishing net filled to capacity, while simultaneously providing a verbal vignette for each image until he had exhausted the family members on display. Not wanting to overstay my welcome, I reached into my back pocket—not to share photographs, but to retrieve my credit card to begin paying for my gas, which at the time averaged about $5.00 per gallon for premium.

Mr. Massey wasn't having it. He insisted on paying for my gas, which exceeded $100 to fill my tank, and he would not accept no for an answer.

I put up a small fight but eventually conceded to his wishes, topped off my vehicle, and then we said our goodbyes as I made my way back to I-85 North.

The course of events made for good conversational material for my wife and me as we drove through the country roads of North Carolina. I also felt a warm sense of pride in knowing that I had done some good in the world and that I had made a difference.

Driving the Wrong Way

My world tour was over, and it was back to the everyday rigors of work for me, which always provided an adventure. I always dreaded the first day back after vacation because it was the toughest.

The longer my vacation, the more difficult it was to get my office whipped back into shape and running like the fine-tuned, well-oiled machine that met my expectations.

However, this time wasn't as bad as others, and we were actually close to achieving our monthly quota. After meeting with my recruiters, I determined we had three prospects for enlistment into the Regular Army and zero prospects for the Army Reserves, and I needed one of each to accomplish my quota.

I learned early that when it comes to sales, the fortune is in the follow-up, meaning the majority of sales are closed after the initial presentation.

This concept was explained to me using an analogy of Red Apples and Green Apples. The red and green apples represent two personality types of buyers. The Red Apple represents the impulsive buyer. These individuals are spontaneous in nature and make quick decisions without thinking things through or weighing all the pros and cons.

Most salesmen love the Red Apple personality type, but they come with their own set of challenges—most detrimental to a recruiter being buyer's remorse. My favorite is the Green Apples!

The Green Apple personality type takes more time to make decisions; however, they are more steadfast once a decision is made and rarely suffer from buyer's remorse. The downside to the Green Apple personality type is that it may take more time for them to ripen, and until then, you must continuously feed them information and find innovative ways to check their disposition—much like a father at a barbecue grill, tending to several steaks simultaneously.

Moving the steaks around on the grill and flipping them over ensures they cook evenly until they are ready to be plated.

Toward the end of each month, if I found myself short of committed prospects for enlistment as we approached the quota deadline, I would perform a ritual of creating a list of potential applicants to call in hopes of engendering a commitment. My preparation process was an entire step-by-step, ritualistic exercise in self-motivation.

I hated telephone prospecting and always used it as a last resort, but over the years I had become very good at getting to the house call. To begin my process, I would completely clear off my desk and wipe it down with Pledge wood cleaner and lemon-scented polish.

I would vigorously buff my desk into a streak-free, high-gloss shine and reorganize my desktop items in a dress-right-dress fashion. I placed my call list at the center of the desk directly in front of where I would be sitting and counter-cornered my phone to the right side of the desk, just short of my fingertips, allowing enough room for my forearm to rest comfortably while dialing numbers quickly and without distraction.

Once everything was strategically placed to my liking, I would set a coaster between my call list and the phone, take a brief moment of admiration, and then make myself a cup of French vanilla creamer and sugar with a splash of coffee. That was the final step of my telephone-prospecting ritual.

Although it is a strong word, I hated telephone prospecting and would do almost anything to avoid sitting down and cold-calling one prospect after another. However, whenever I committed to slowing down, taking my time, and making the calls, I always made appointments. This day was no different from any other before.

After a few warm-up calls, I began making appointments and assigning them to my recruiters to be conducted that very day. I was never taught hate growing up, and as an adult in the military, I took every opportunity to make a point to my light-green counterparts that there are both good and bad people, regardless of skin color.

After a few more calls, I reestablished contact with a really good kid who had not been ready to make a commitment to the Army during his initial appointment. It appeared I had followed up at the right time, because he was now ready to enlist.

I immediately went through the pre-qualification procedures and scheduled an appointment for later that same day.

After capturing all the necessary information, I observed one of my recruiters—whom I affectionately nicknamed "Crusty" because of his advanced age. From the large picture window directly in front of my desk, centered on the wall to the right of the door that led out to the main office, was where the assigned recruiters sat.

Crusty and I got along a little better than the other Light Green soldiers the Army placed under my leadership. However, he still held a few preconceived notions about what Army culture referred to during that time as Dark Green soldiers. Armed with the prospect's information, I called out to Crusty and asked him to join me in my office so I could brief him before sending him out to close the deal on what would be the final enlistment needed to meet my monthly quota.

After receiving his marching orders, Crusty gathered his things, donned his headgear, and ranger-walked to his government vehicle, his feet barely touching the ground. I exited my office and stepped into the bullpen to watch him drive out of the parking lot.

He made a few turns to enter traffic and soon disappeared among the other vehicles on the road.

A few hours later, Crusty whipped his government-assigned vehicle into the parking lot and slammed the gear selector into park. He then briskly walked through the door of the recruiting station, happier than I had ever seen him before.

After placing his gear on his desk, he beelined to my office to share the good news. The young man had agreed to enlist, and his commitment would close out the station for the month. We would achieve our monthly quota three months in a row, which would make many people throughout our chain of command happy. Crusty finished sharing his good news, and then his tone shifted just before he announced that he wanted to share additional information with me about his appointment.

He explained how embarrassed he was; however, he felt compelled to share his story with me, believing that the humor in it highlighted his inner fears and illuminated a powerful lesson for him that day. After preparing me for what he was about to say, I was all in, and he had my undivided attention.

Despite conducting his appointment in a low-income housing project populated predominantly by Black people and other minorities, he described— in vivid detail—the beauty of the day. As he continued setting up his story and pulling me further into his words, he painted a picture of Carolina blue skies, warm weather, and a steady breeze blowing off the Neuse River. Crusty described the feeling he had as he walked to his car, started the engine, and buckled his seatbelt. Because the day was so beautiful, he decided to drive with the windows down to take advantage of the nearly perfect temperature.

All set; he put the car in gear and began his drive back to the recruiting station to share his good news. As he drove down the street between the project homes, he noticed he was the only person on the road.

He wasn't bothered by it. He let his left arm rest partially out the window while his right hand remained at the twelve-o'clock position on the steering wheel. It was so quiet and peaceful that he could hear the rubber of his tires gripping the asphalt as he continued driving with all four windows rolled down.

At this point in his story, I was sitting on the edge of my seat, with no idea where he was going with it.

He then said that someone ran out of their apartment and yelled out to him, "HEY!" Crusty went on to share the fear he felt as one person after another ran out of their doors, yelling at him as he drove down the street between the project homes. As his fear increased, he sped up, driving faster and faster with a heightened sense of anxiety, as if he were being chased and in potential danger.

It was the instinctive physiological response to a threatening situation—fight or flight. With his heart racing and a heightened state of awareness from the excessive amount of adrenaline flowing through his body, Crusty reached the end of the street to exit the neighborhood, where he instantly felt like an idiot. Posted on a wooden telephone pole on the corner was a sign that read *One Way*. The telling of the event from his perspective was hysterical.

Once Crusty reached the climax of his story, we shared side-splitting laughs, as if a professional comedian had delivered a punchline to an arena filled to capacity.

Laughing from relief, embarrassment, and his self-inflicted fear—rooted in discomfort with people of color—caused me to feel a degree of sadness. The Army does a good job of bringing together the melting pot of America under one banner for the purpose of defending the nation.

However, there are still many small subcultures within the organization that tug at the fabric of an acronym that guided my supervisory decision-making process.

During my twenty-year tenure, that acronym was LDRSHIP. LDRSHIP was a play on the word *leadership* and stood for Loyalty, Duty, Respect, Service, Honor, Integrity, and Personal Courage.

I found it ironic that we both felt a sense of uneasiness around a majority of the other race—but for very different reasons.

CHAPTER NINE
Three Fifty-Seven

Each year, the Army publishes a list of senior Non-Commissioned Officers to be promoted to the next grade or rank, using an elaborate system of promotion numbers and zones, such as primary and secondary. I was always driven by ambition and determination to move up to the next level. Although joining the military was not my first choice in life, it ended up becoming my only choice, and my goal was to make the best of the opportunity.

That particular year, I felt secure and very confident that I would make the promotion list. Still, I tried not to allow the thought to consume me, choosing instead to remain focused on the job at hand and let the rest fall into place. Over the years, I had become quite regimented and stuck closely to my daily pregame work rituals. The night before, I would lay out my uniform, including my dress socks, white T-shirt, black patent leather with Honor Guard edge dressing, and ensure all my awards, badges, and decorations were in their rightful places before going to bed.

When my alarm clock went off—as it did every morning at 0600 hours—I sat at the edge of the bed, silenced the alarm, and took a few seconds to gather myself.

After cycling through my preparatory steps in the dark so as not to wake my wife, I gave her a soft kiss on the cheek and whispered that I loved her and would talk to her later. Taking extra care not to wake her completely, I exited the house, pulling the door closed slowly and waiting to hear the click of the latch as it passed the strike plate, before gently closing the screen door.

One of the best parts of my day was the ride to work. Although it was short in distance and lacked the start-and-stop traffic of a big city, I made up for it with my morning theatrics. Once I reached the edge of the neighborhood, I would turn my music up to a decibel just above loud to get the day started. After passing the sentry and entering the civilian population beyond the security of the military installation—aside from an occasional stoplight—the Shell gas station would be my first stop of the day.

As a creature of habit, I parked in the same spot near the front door, placed the car in park, turned off the ignition, exited the vehicle, and pressed the lock button on the key fob as I entered the convenience store. Rarely did I miss a day, and you could set your clock by my arrival. The clerk and I would always exchange the greeting of the day before I beelined to the coffee section.

I would pull a large cup from the dispenser, add two French vanilla creamers and four sugars, and then fill it to the rim. I always grabbed two straws and fanned them out to stir my coffee until I was satisfied that all the sugar had dissolved and the creamer was properly mixed. I would take a small sip—being careful not to burn my tongue, but just enough to perform my personal taste test. Once satisfied, I would put a lid on the cup before heading to the counter to request a box of Black and Mild cigars—an ugly habit I had picked up to deal with my nervous energy and the day-to-day emotional roller coaster of being a Station Commander of an Army Recruiting Station.

I took a great deal of pride in my military career, and I made it a habit to always lead from the front.

This meant that most days I would be the first soldier in the office and the last to leave at the end of the day. After reaching the parking lot of the recruiting station, I would back my car into the parking space and exit the vehicle with my coffee in hand.

After unlocking the station door, I would do a walkthrough and turn on all the lights before returning to the front of the station. Once outside, I would push the door completely open until it stayed open on its own. I would remove my beret and stuff it behind my belt on the right side of my waist, between the first and second belt loops of my pants. I would then set my coffee on the bricks protruding from the wall below the window seal, under the large picture window to the left of the open door, before removing the box of Black and Mild and a lighter from my pocket.

I would stand there drinking my coffee with one hand and puffing my cheap cigar with the other until the sun rose and my soldiers began to arrive one by one. Every morning began the same way—from the moment I woke up until the last soldier crossed the office threshold. After that, no two days were ever alike.

Sergeant Bailey was the first soldier to report to work that day, and he appeared unusually enthusiastic.

We both exchanged our morning pleasantries as he walked past me to enter the office. I immediately sensed he had something up his sleeve because the smirk on his face gave him away—he had a terrible poker face.

I could always tell when he was up to something; I only needed to wait for the other shoe to drop. As if he wanted an audience, Bailey announced in my direction, "Congratulations!" Unsure where he was going with this, I responded, "Congratulations for what?" He then shared some very good news that I was unaware of. The night before, the Department of the Army had released the promotion list. Soldiers around the world waited for the list to be published at midnight; however, I had chosen to go to bed, stick to my ritual, and check the list from work the next day. All the suspense and anticipation were ruined as Bailey filled me in on my good fortune. "You made the promotion list; your number is three-hundred and fifty-seven."

I thanked him for sharing the good news, but little did I know it was a setup for what he planned to say next.

Before I finished my sentence, he delivered the news he really wanted to share. "Aren't you going to congratulate me?"

I quickly replied, "Congratulate you for what?"—a response I now realize played right into a plan he had clearly rehearsed. He then shared with me, and the rest of the office, that he had also made the promotion list. Unlike me, his promotion sequence number was number two. In an effort to belittle me in front of the other soldiers, he asked the question he had been saving for his finale. "Do you know what that means?"

Knowing he wanted to make his point in a clever but sarcastic way, I obliged him, hoping he would get to what he was after so we could move on with our day. I answered, "What does it mean?"

He replied, "It means that I will outrank you and no longer have to take orders from you!" Shocked by his comment, I quickly educated him on the difference between rank and authority by position before retreating to my office to prepare for our morning huddle and start the duty day.

During this time period in the Army, there were a few things soldiers had to accomplish before they could receive their promotions.

First was the wait for the Army to announce the sequence numbers for the soldiers who had been identified as promotable. Second was the requirement to complete the appropriate leadership course for the next level of promotion.

Within a month of being notified that I had made the promotion list, I found myself attending the Advanced Non-Commissioned Officers Course (ANCOC) in preparation for my promotion. The only thing left for me to do after that was wait for my sequence number—357—to come up so I could receive my promotion.

Failed APFT

After graduating from ANCOC, I returned to my recruiting station, and it was business as usual on the heels of another successful month of quota achievement. I received a call from my supervisor informing me that it was now Bailey's opportunity to attend ANCOC; however, I was tasked with administering his Army Physical Fitness Test (APFT). In the early 2000s, the APFT consisted of two minutes of push-ups, two minutes of sit-ups, and a two-mile run.

Although I was ordered to administer Bailey's fitness exam, I made a command decision to delegate the task to Crusty, with the assistance of another Sergeant under my leadership. I called Crusty into my office and provided him with a blank physical fitness (PT) form to record Bailey's scores for each event.

Bailey went home to change out of his uniform in preparation for the exam and agreed to meet the other Sergeants at the designated location. We would all meet back at the station later that evening.

Off they went, and I didn't think much more about it. A few hours passed, and they all returned like horses at feeding time after roaming a pasture all day.

Crusty handed me the completed form with Bailey's recorded PT scores, and I immediately knew something was off. Bailey was not the pillar of fitness, nor did he present the image one typically envisions when hearing the word, *Soldier*. Standing in my office, face-to-face with fabricated scores in my hand, I looked Crusty in the eyes and asked, "Did he pass his PT test?"

Crusty quickly replied, "Oh yes, Sarge—he did good," and then made a hasty retreat to his desk.

I noticed the younger Sergeant avoiding eye contact, so I quickly called him into my office and asked him to close the door behind him.

"Have a seat, Sarge."

After getting comfortable, he asked, "What's up, Sarge?" I knew I would have to up the ante to uncover the truth and confirm my suspicion of deception.

"Sarge, I am only going to ask you this one time. If I find out you are lying to me, I will take whatever disciplinary action I can to deal with your dishonesty!" He didn't put up much of a fight and folded in less time than it took me to complete my condensed, threatening monologue.

He began his descent and came in for a landing to reveal the truth I knew was being held from me. After issuing my threat, I was careful to ease up on the harshness of my demeanor and make the Sergeant feel comfortable so I could ascertain the maximum amount of information possible. He came out of the gate fast. "Sarge, it was really bad," he said. "When he popped cork, I knew it was bad."

At that moment, I realized I had become one of those Old Heads I had talked about earlier in my tenure. "Popped cork—what do you mean?" I asked. Although this was a very serious matter, his explanation of cork popping was as funny as any illustration I had heard at the time.

In the rigid structure of the military, the Army Physical Fitness Test was always conducted in the order of push-ups, sit-ups, and a two-mile run. The young Sergeant shared with me that he had been holding Bailey's feet during the sit-up event.

What he shared next still activates my immaturity and causes me to chuckle, even to this day. About ten sit-ups in, Bailey lost control and released flatulence with the young Sergeant's head in close proximity. Until that day, I had never heard the term "popping cork." Popping cork, as it relates to the APFT, means a soldier passing gas while executing sit-ups. After the young Sergeant explained the meaning of popping cork, we laughed until we were out of breath and tears flowed from our eyes.

I had a tough time regaining my composure, but I had to set my laughter aside to deal with the more serious issue of a soldier under my leadership failing his physical fitness exam—along with the collective planning and execution of a cover-up.

The rules and regulations of the U.S. Army did a good job of mitigating many potential racial issues, but another trait that is essential among soldiers is trust. Without it, very little can be accomplished. After a brief moment of contemplation, I called Crusty into my office, figuring that my career-threatening statement had worked so well the first time that I would use it again.

Like a broken record, I repeated the same exact words I had said to the younger Sergeant earlier, and Crusty took the bait. He was relieved to have come clean with the truth. Because they had lied, I made the decision to have Crusty retest Bailey; this time, he would use my camera to record the event. With not much time left before close of business, Crusty agreed to bring the camera to my home at the conclusion of the physical fitness retest. Arriving home, getting comfortable, and having dinner with my family, I heard Crusty's rusted truck muffler as his engine idled in my driveway before he shut it off.

Then came a knock at the door. I opened it to find Crusty on the other side of the screen door holding my camera, asking if I would meet him around back of my living quarters in military housing so we could sit on the screened-in patio and talk more about the events of the day. It came as no surprise that Bailey had failed his physical fitness exam again, and now I had to figure out what my next move would be.

Unlike many of the light-green leaders I had encountered in the past, I believed in the structure, rules, and regulations of the Army and sought to assist any soldier under my leadership, regardless of race, creed, or color.

The funny thing is, the Army did not teach me that. Ironically, I was taught to love all people by a woman who lived through an extreme amount of racism in the Jim Crow South. With a deep, unspoken, and unsubstantiated understanding of Bailey's disdain for me, it was in my core to do whatever I could to help my soldier through what I imagined was a traumatizing period in his life.

You will never get rich serving our country, but a promotion can be life-altering for a military family. The next morning, I called our First Sergeant to seek leadership counseling and advice.

I explained the course of events to our leadership and was given two courses of action. Ultimately, it was up to me to decide which direction I would take, keeping in mind that I held this soldier's career in the palm of my hand.

The decision I was about to make had long-lasting, life-altering implications, and as a leader, it was important to me that I did what was best for my soldier and his family. My first alternative was to turn a blind eye and allow Bailey to report to his leadership course, fail his PT test, and forfeit his promotion.

My second option was to recommend an alternate school date to provide my soldier additional time to get himself in better shape, pass his PT test, and receive his promotion after completing the required leadership course. It didn't take me long to decide. I called our leadership to inform them of my desire to give Bailey more time to get in shape and asked if his reporting date could be changed.

Word came back quickly. Staff Sergeant Bailey's reporting date was pushed back a few months so he would be better prepared and given the best opportunity to receive his next promotion.

Feeling confident that I had made the right decision, I called Bailey into my office and sat him down to explain what provisions had been made on his behalf.

Although I knew he cared little for me, I felt good about my decision. It was made void of racism and prejudice. Still, it saddened me to know that if the roles were reversed, he would not have done the same for me.

Lawn Ritual

During the summer months, I made every attempt to cut my lawn on Saturday mornings, but due to my heavy work schedule, it seemed nearly impossible to keep that timeline. As a result, Sunday afternoon became my weekly grass-cutting ritual. Directly across the street from me lived a Marine I befriended during my first week in the neighborhood. My wife and I had relocated from Charlotte, North Carolina, and coincidentally, Charlotte was his hometown. He vowed that once he retired from the Marine Corps, he and his family planned on settling back there. We would stand out in the middle of the street for hours, talking about Charlotte and the home he planned to build for his family once he hung up his boots for good.

The Gunnery Sergeant and I never stepped foot in each other's quarters; however, we got along well.

He would always speak to my wife when we would leave or return home each day. I made sure to reciprocate his kind Southern gesture by acknowledging his wife and two small children whenever I was present to witness their comings and goings. Most of the time, he would one-up me by bringing me a cold beer whenever he saw me out in the sun cutting my grass. Although I didn't like beer, I always thanked him for his generosity and drank it down as if it were my favorite beverage—which is a nice, cold glass of sweet tea.

That Sunday afternoon, I was unable to finish priming my lawnmower before my neighbor beelined across the street with two cold beers in one hand and a bottle opener in the other. After handing me one of the beers, he quickly opened his and passed the bottle opener to me, and I did the same. He made quick work of the small talk, clearly trying to move the conversation along.

I began to sense that my neighbor had something he needed to tell me, and he wasted little time getting to it.

Because he was unfamiliar with the differences between the Army's rank structure and the U.S. Marine Corps, he always called me *Gunny*, which was short for Gunnery Sergeant—the equivalent rank in our respective branches of service. His opening statement, in an effort to clear his conscience, began with, "Gunny, I don't know how to tell you this."

He went on to explain that a few days earlier, he and his family had joined other relatives in supporting their sons at a Pop Warner football game. His son and Bailey's son played on the same team and sat in close proximity to one another in the bleachers during the game.

Although he too was a Caucasian man, I could see the disgust on his face as he prepared to deliver the main course of the conversation he had been building toward. The Gunnery Sergeant began his final descent by apologizing in advance for what my soldier and his spouse had publicly said in an attempt to defame my character.

He went above and beyond to assure me that neither he nor his family were cut from the same cloth of ignorance and prejudice. His intro was so long that it caused my demeanor to reflect what I was saying to myself, which was, *"Come on with the story already!"*

211

Only after I made him feel comfortable—by assuring him that I believed he was nothing like my soldier and that I would not judge him for the color of his skin or the mistakes of someone else—did he finally lower his wheels and bring the plane in for a landing.

With much caution, he told me how my soldier and his wife sat in the bleachers at a Pop Warner football game and called me several names. They were angry because I had his leadership course date pushed back to give him additional time to get in better shape—a decision that ultimately saved his career.

All the names my soldier and his spouse chose to call me—and believe me, they were all bad—one really stuck with me the most.

If I am being honest, I did not care much for my soldier either; however, I would never publicly call him or any of my soldiers out of their names or use my grade or position to deliberately derail anyone's career. It doesn't take a brain surgeon to figure out which racial epithet my soldier and his spouse chose to weaponize, and yes, it was the word Nigger. I would love to tell you that it didn't hurt, but I would be lying if I did so.

As a parent, I am guilty of teaching my children the nursery rhyme *sticks and stones may break my bones, but words will never hurt me*. However, I no longer believe in nursery rhymes and have learned that words have power—and sometimes they do hurt, a lot. What started slowly ended swiftly, and before I knew it, I was thanking my neighbor for sharing his confession.

His story was very enlightening and left me feeling numb, similar to the tingling of neuropathy in your lower extremities—only the numbness seemed to be in my head.

With the lawnmower, gas can, and other lawn equipment scattered across the front lawn, I sat down on my front porch for a while to finish my beer and process the information I had just received. Still processing what my soldier and his wife had done, I came to my feet, started my lawnmower, and made overlapping passes from one end of the lawn to the other until the entire lawn was cut. I spent what was left of my weekend considering different methods of dealing with the situation, but I was unable to think of anything that felt suitable. Given that I had never dealt with a situation like this before, I decided that I would do nothing.

Friendship Bread

Somehow, word had gotten out, and my soldier and his spouse learned that I had become aware of their behavior and their public, hateful racial rant during their son's Pop Warner football games. At the start of every morning, I conducted a one-on-one meeting with each of my soldiers, one directly after the other. These meetings normally lasted about fifteen to thirty minutes, depending on the amount of new business generated the previous week.

This system was developed by the United States Army Recruiting Command (USAREC) and was called the Daily Performance Review, affectionately nicknamed *DPR* by the soldiers assigned to recruiting.

The DPR process was a step-by-step method used to establish command and control, as well as to gain and maintain awareness of prospects and applicants in the recruiting station pipeline for enlistment preparation and processing, keeping pace with the fast tempo of Army recruiting.

The days were long and moved quickly, as the months seemed to fly by. Mondays usually proved the most informative and set the tone for the rest of the week.

Each Station Commander put their own personal spin on the DPR procedure, while still adhering to how it was taught, in an effort to ascertain the information deemed most important to accomplish the mission and keep higher headquarters off our backs. I, on the other hand, loved to add my own personal touches to any process I believed to be linear.

I standardized my own DPR sessions, and with consistency, they became second nature over the course of several years.

First, I would give the greeting of the day, followed by asking my soldiers about their spouses and children, if they had any. After the pleasantries, I would then get down to business and start asking questions about the disposition of past prospects and applicants in the civilian circle—this was known as "old business." Without missing a beat, I would roll directly into "new business," followed by asking if my help or assistance was needed in getting a prospect across the finish line.

Finally, I would ask my recruiters if they had any questions for me, inform them of my availability, and wish them well by saying, "Have a great recruiting day!"

During Monday's DPR session with Crusty, he shared a conversation he had with Bailey and his wife over coffee and cake the weekend prior. I managed to maintain my poise and make it to the end of the week, as Friday was rapidly approaching. I recall feeling good about the upcoming weekend because I had an unusual Saturday off, which was a rarity during this time in my career.

Friday morning came just as fast as the day before it. I woke and followed my dependable courses of action in preparation for the start of my day.

As usual, I arrived at the office first, opened the doors, and turned on the lights, then returned to the front of the office to continue enjoying the coffee I had purchased from the corner gas station moments earlier. However, this day was different from the rest. Bailey arrived at work earlier than he had in the past and requested to have a word with me before the other recruiters arrived.

Although I was aware of the content, he was about to share with me, I worked very hard to suppress the fact that I had already been tipped off by Crusty during our DPR session earlier that week.

He began telling me what happened during his son's football game, partially throwing his wife under the bus as he eventually worked his way toward a lackluster apology for calling me a racial epithet during his son's football game, while making every attempt to intercede on his wife's behalf. Bailey spoke of his wife's feelings of regret for her actions and put me on notice that she would be arriving soon to offer me an apology in person.

He did all he could to prepare me for his spouse's arrival that morning. His conversation felt more like a plea for me to show his wife some grace when she arrived rather than a sincere apology for their despicable behavior. I assured him that I would be nothing less than respectful to his wife and would not replicate the behavior they had displayed toward me. Although I believed that if there were ever a time for me to let loose, this was it.

Shortly after our conversation, Mrs. Bailey drove up and sat in her car at the back of the parking lot.

I noticed her immediately because she left her engine running and headlights on as she waited for her husband to provide some type of signal indicating it was alright for her to approach the office. I could tell by the timing of events and how everything was unfolding that this was a poorly planned—and even more poorly executed—operation to counterbalance their public perception and attitude toward me and, ultimately, ease the embarrassment of being viewed in the community as racist.

Eventually, Bailey noticed his wife sitting in the back of the parking lot and exited the office to accompany her inside to apologize to her husband's supervisor, whom she had called a Nigger just a few days earlier.

I sat behind my desk, watching them through the picture window of my office, second only to the storefront windows that led out to the parking lot just beyond the sidewalk. As they got closer to the entrance, I walked out of my office in the back to greet my soldier's wife. Like a true Southern gentleman, he opened the door for his wife to enter the building.

She walked through the door carrying what appeared to be a cake on a plate covered with Saran Wrap, held in both of her hands. If I had to choose an animal to describe her personality, it would be a Doberman Pinscher—not the large ones with long legs, pointed ears, and intimidating teeth, but the miniature kind. She was a very small woman in stature, but what she lacked in size she made up for in attitude. We met in the center of the office, forming a triangle, with Mrs. Bailey and me facing one another and my soldier standing an equal distance between us, to my right and her to my left.

With nervous energy, I rendered my soldier and his other half the greeting of the day, although I felt neither of them deserved one moment of my time. "Good morning, how are you?" I said enthusiastically. She replied and went directly into her apology. Once she finished offering it, she explained what she was holding.

She told me it was Friendship Bread and that she had been up late baking it for me, extending her arms and gesturing for me to take it. I graciously extended my hands and assumed control of the plate. As I positioned my hands underneath it, I thanked Mrs. Bailey for the Friendship Bread.

We said our goodbyes, and I retreated to my office. I walked away fuming with anger. I could not believe she would call me a racial epithet just days earlier and then prepare food for me, as if I would trust her enough to consume anything she had made. Bailey opened the door leading out to the parking lot and walked his wife to her car. I watched them exchange a few words as he opened her car door, leaned inside, and kissed her before walking back into the office and taking a seat at his desk. As soon as my feet crossed the threshold of my office door, I placed the plate of Friendship Bread on the top left corner at the edge of my desk. I wanted to ensure it was out of the way and would not become a distraction during my upcoming DPR sessions.

I sat at my desk preparing for my sessions, replaying the incident in my mind like a scene on repeat. Even now, I'm not sure how I made it through without losing my composure, offending anyone, or making a mistake that could have jeopardized my career.

Overall, I believe I handled the situation as best I could. I wish I could say this was the first time I had been called a racial epithet, but this time was different and extremely difficult to deal with.

I had never been called a racial epithet by someone who worked for me—someone whose career I had fought to help advance. I took a few deep breaths to gather myself in preparation for the rest of my day.

My mindset was simple: the world was not going to stop turning on its axis because a Caucasian had called me the N-word. I pressed on as if nothing had happened and restarted my morning rituals previously interrupted by my soldier and his spouse. I organized my desk, ensuring everything was in its rightful place, analyzed the productivity of my soldier from the previous week, and finally prepared my talking points for each soldier. Bailey usually fell somewhere in the middle of my DPR lineup, but on this day, I called an audible, placing him last in the rotation. The truth is, I really did not want to speak to him at all!

However, I believed I had an obligation that was greater than both of us, so the show had to go on. One after the other, soldiers entered my office, closing the door behind them and setting up their laptops along with any documents needed for discussion during our DPR sessions.

Just as quickly as I settled into my routine and found my stride, I began to feel the uneasiness of anxiety—it was time for me to sit down with Bailey and conduct his DPR session. As I completed my sessions with the other soldiers, I sent them out into the community one by one.

I had a philosophy I acquired from an older soldier many years earlier when I was a young Private stationed overseas in Europe.

He would always say, "If you don't have anything to do, don't do it around here!" I found the phrase extremely fitting for this occasion because a recruiter is useless sitting in the office when there is a limited-to-nonexistent walk-in market. I took a drink of my lukewarm coffee before notifying Bailey that I was ready. He walked into my office disheveled, as usual, with his arms filled with documents and his laptop.

He always painted the illusion that he had a lot going on; however, I always knew he did just enough to get by. I imagined he was also in a precarious situation, working for a dark-green soldier, praying for my downfall but also needing to protect his livelihood to provide for his family.

After settling in, I proceeded with our session no differently than I had in the past. I quickly looked him over to ensure his uniform was up to par. I stressed the importance of appearance because I believe there is nothing worse than a raggedy soldier.

Without delay, I kicked the meeting into high gear by asking him how he was doing.

I always began my sessions by establishing and maintaining rapport with my soldiers. I felt it was important to ask questions about them and their families' well-being.

My line of questioning also served as icebreakers, which we both needed due to the racial tension that filled the room. Next, I asked about his son and his wife as if I had not seen nor spoken to her in years. He talked a little about his son, sharing his excitement about how well he was catching on to the game of football.

I sat patiently, listening and waiting for him to reach the bridge of his point so I could chime in with my chorus and move this intricate process along, extracting the information I needed to lead my team to success. I hit all my points one after the other, guiding our session with the precision of a highly skilled surgeon.

Guiding the old-business portion of the DPR from my list of potential applicants, we made quick work of that phase and transitioned into new business without much thought. Our discussion about new business flowed effortlessly as I asked a predetermined group of questions and provided guidance for follow-ups.

At the conclusion of all my DPR sessions, I always ended with a question that was quickly followed by a statement once the answer was provided. Without breaking momentum, I asked Bailey, "Do you have anything for me?" He quickly answered, "No, Sergeant!" Under normal circumstances, I would have fired back just as quickly with my parting statement, but this day was far from normal. Throughout the entire DPR session, I had been thinking of a way to express my disgust and anger toward him and his wife for calling me a Nigger, and I drew a blank until that exact moment.

He, too, was conditioned to my method of ending meetings, and sensing the end was near, he closed his laptop and waited to be dismissed. I then leaned forward and extended my left arm to the top left corner of my desk, my fingers extended and joined, palm perpendicular to the wall.

With a stern look of repulsion on my face as I locked eyes with him, I swiped my hand across the desk, sliding his wife's Friendship Bread off the edge.

Positioned on the floor directly below the edge of my desk was an empty gray metal trash can.

Without blinking an eye, I maintained my stare as the plate hit the bottom of the trash can, making a sound equivalent to throwing a brick through a storefront picture window.

I could see his temples flex and his jaws tighten as he ground his teeth together, but there was nothing he could do. I think he knew he had it coming. Right on cue, I delivered my final statement—the one that always signaled the end of my meetings. "Have a nice day!"

He gathered his things, exited my office, and departed the recruiting station for a day of prospecting in the community.

We never spoke about the events of that day, and it was business as usual going forward. And to this day, I have never eaten Friendship Bread.

Promotion Time

After safeguarding my soldier's career and having him and his wife call me a racial epithet in the presence of a small coastal Carolina community, I was sent to what was then called Fort Jackson to attend the Advanced Non-Commissioned Officers Course, which was a prerequisite course required to obtain my next promotion.

Upon successfully completing the advanced leadership course, I returned to my recruiting station, rolled up my sleeves, and quickly got back to work. I immediately sensed a deep-seated feeling of bitterness toward me from my soldier—most likely because I had completed a major step toward my promotion while his start date had been altered because he had allowed himself to get out of shape. Although tension between us was evident, we both pushed forward, doing what we needed to do to make it through together.

The Army is structured into different levels of accountability and leadership, from the highest level down to the individual soldier.

In the United States Army Recruiting Command, the levels of leadership followed a similar structure: Recruiting Station, Recruiting Company, Recruiting Battalion, and Recruiting Command.

At the end of each fiscal-year quarter, the Battalion would bring together soldiers from six Recruiting Companies to provide training, present awards, and promote those who had met all requirements and received promotion orders from the Department of the Army. Unlike the initial promotion list with sequence numbers, Bailey was not privy to this notification.

My First Sergeant called to inform me that I would be promoted during our next Battalion training exercise. Christmas was rapidly approaching, and that year's training was held the week before December 25th.

Although my official promotion wasn't until January 1st, the decision was made to recognize me in the presence of my peers almost a week ahead of my actual date of rank. Armed with the advance notice of my impending promotion, I decided to take vacation beginning the day after my promotion ceremony and extending until a week after the New Year. I was over the moon with excitement.

Battalion training sessions typically lasted a few days and were held in a major North Carolina metropolitan area.

They were always a good time for networking and fellowshipping with other recruiters and Station Commanders from across the state—many of whom you may not have seen or spoken to in quite some time. I enjoyed most Battalion training sessions, but this one promised to be special. This was the day I had worked so hard for and, to be honest, it seemed nearly impossible when I thought back to September 1988, when I first enlisted in the Army as a last resort in life.

My wife and first-born son accompanied me to a large ballroom filled to capacity. Earlier that same year, I had been informed by Bailey my sequence number was 357. I can still hear the condescending tone in his voice as he shared his own sequence number of 2 and assured me that he would be promoted before me, no longer having to take orders from me because he would then outrank me.

I found myself sitting at the front of the room with my wife and son, bubbling with anticipation of what was to come. The Battalion Commander announced to the room that he was going to promote a soldier that day and called my family and me to the front.

With my family facing the audience, the Battalion Commander and the Command Sergeant Major removed the rank insignias from my uniform and threw them both on the floor just before I heard the following words.

ATTENTION TO ORDERS! The Secretary of the Army has reposed special trust and confidence in the patriotism, valor, fidelity, and professional excellence of John I Payne Jr. In view of these qualities and his demonstrated leadership potential and dedicated service to the United States Army, he is, therefore, promoted from Staff Sergeant to Sergeant First Class. Promotion is effective 1 January 2001 with a date of rank of 1 January 2001.

After the reading of the orders, my wife assisted the Sergeant Major in affixing the new rank insignias in place of the old ones that had been removed and thrown on the floor moments earlier. As a congratulatory gesture, soldiers were encouraged to line up and shake my hand at the conclusion of the promotion ceremony. I can't recall everyone who passed in front of me extending their hand, but I will never forget the look on Bailey's face or the sour-grapes tone of his voice, void of inflection. He extended his hand, said "Congratulations," and kept moving without breaking his stride.

Once the pleasantries ended, my wife and I—with our son in tow—departed to enjoy what turned out to be a great holiday season. Not long after the change of seasons that year, the Recruiting Company was disbanded, and my soldiers and I were reassigned to other locations in accordance with the needs of the Army. Although things are much different now, I did go on to win every award the U.S. Army Recruiting Command had to offer and later retired after twenty years of honorable service to the United States of America.

Havelock Recruiting Station 1999 - 2002

ATTENTION TO ORDERS! *To all who shall see these presents, greeting: This is to certify that John Isham Payne, Jr. Sergeant First Class Regular Army having served faithfully and honorably, was retired from the United States Army on the First day of October Two Thousand and Eight.*

CERTIFICATE OF RETIREMENT
FROM THE ARMED FORCES OF THE UNITED STATES OF AMERICA

To all who shall see these presents, greeting:
This is to certify that

JOHN HLIAM PAYNE, JR. SERGEANT FIRST CLASS, REGULAR ARMY

having served faithfully and honorably,
was retired from the

UNITED STATES ARMY

on the **FIRST** day of **OCTOBER**
TWO THOUSAND AND EIGHT.

Washington, D.C.

GENERAL, UNITED STATES ARMY
CHIEF OF STAFF

The U.S. Army Recruiter Ring is a prestigious, custom-made yellow gold ring awarded to elite recruiters for exceptional performance. The ring signifies inclusion among the Army's top-tier recruiters and stands as a lasting mark of excellence within the recruiting force.

The U.S. Army Gold Recruiter Badge is a prestigious award presented to active-duty personnel serving in the U.S. Army Recruiting Command (USAREC) who demonstrate sustained, high-level recruiting success. The badge signifies superior performance, consistency, and excellence in mission accomplishment.

The Glen E. Morrell Award consist of a medallion and ring. It is the absolute ultimate achievement award offered by the U.S. Army recruiting Command for recruiting excellence.

To everyone who picks up this book,

If you find the lesson here doesn't immediately resonate, remember this: when you encounter adversity—be it racism, prejudice, injustice, persecution, or attacks on your character—know that you have a Father in Jesus who is always ready to fight for you, if only you learn to Stand Down. Over time, I've realized that not every battle is ours to fight. Since the dawn of time, our Father has never lost a battle. So, before you try to handle things on your own, pause and let Him work. You may find that He will prepare a place of honor for you, even in the presence of those who oppose you.

Dr. John I. Payne Jr., US Army (Ret)

www.ingramcontent.com/pod-product-compliance
Ingram Content Group UK Ltd.
Pitfield, Milton Keynes, MK11 3LW, UK
UKHW020240240426
12049UKWH00026B/185/J